FYODOR DOSTOEVSKY

FYODOR DOSTOEVSKY

A CRITICAL STUDY

BY

J. MIDDLETON MURRY

NEW YORK / RUSSELL & RUSSELL

1966

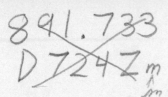
FIRST PUBLISHED IN 1924
REISSUED, 1966, BY RUSSELL & RUSSELL
A DIVISION OF ATHENEUM HOUSE, INC.
L.C. CATALOG CARD NO: 66—24737

TO
GORDON CAMPBELL

REPRINTED FROM A COPY IN THE COLLECTIONS OF
THE COLUMBIA UNIVERSITY LIBRARIES

PRINTED IN THE UNITED STATES OF AMERICA

PREFACE

" I do not speak," said Dostoevsky in the
famous speech on Pushkin which was the end
of the work of his life, " as a literary critic;
I am only thinking of what may be for us prophetic in his work."

It would be foolish for an English writer to
attempt a purely literary criticism of Dostoevsky's work; this book also professes only to
think of what may be for us prophetic in it.
Dostoevsky is a phenomenon which has lately
burst upon our astonished minds, one towards
which an attitude must be determined quickly,
almost at the peril of our souls. Our English
literature has lately emerged from a period
during which French influence upon it has been
palpable. But the influence of the French has
been slight and mainly confined to externals;
there has not been sufficient force in the French
literature of the nineteenth century to make
its influence more deeply felt. Dostoevsky
is a different matter. He is a power where

influence may well be incalculable, not upon the form—he never achieved his own form— but upon the thought and spirit of our literature.

An English critic who is ignorant of the Russian language can derive very little help towards a comprehension of Dostoevsky from any other books than Dostoevsky's own. There is in English only one book that is illuminating —the translation of Dmitri Merejhkovsky's *Tolstoi as Man and Artist*, which contains some profound chapters upon Dostoevsky's work. Apparently when it was published, fifteen years ago, it met with no success, so that the second part, *The Religion of Dostoevsky*, was never translated. It would have been invaluable. One cannot say the same of another Russian criticism which has lately been translated: *Dostoevsky : His Life and Literary Activity*, by Evgeny Soloviev, which is spiteful, shallow and misleading. Perhaps this lack of authorities has done no harm. Dostoevsky, like all great writers, affords his own best commentary, and in any case this book does not profess to expound Dostoevsky from any other than a purely English, even insular, point of view. In a sense it has been pioneer work, and if the trail has at times for want of company seemed a lonely one, the writer has taken heart from a letter which Dostoevsky wrote in the last year of his life : —

I swear to you that though I have received much recognition, possibly more than I deserve, still the critics, the literary critics, who certainly have often —no, rather, very seldom—praised me, nevertheless have always spoken of me so lightly and superficially that I am obliged to assume that all those things which my heart brought forth in pain and tribulation, and which came directly from my soul, have simply passed unperceived. . . .

There it stands on Dostoevsky's authority that his own works are the only road to an understanding of his thought. There is no single aspect of his thought which is not reflected faithfully and imaginatively expressed in his novels. It could only have been expressed in imaginative terms, not because it is more mystical than any living thought must be, but because the strange characteristic which distinguishes it is the intimacy of its relation to human life. Abstract thought and conduct have always been divorced in the West, since the day when the Father of Philosophy pronounced that the theoretic life was the best of all. Fundamental to Dostoevsky is a new and passionate synthesis of thought and life. Never has the ideal world been brought so close to the real as in his works ; they do not merely march with each other, they are confounded and they are one. Other writers have created their figures against a metaphysical background, it is true ; but in Dostoevsky's work the figures themselves are the metaphysical background. *Cogito ergo sum* is the principle of their being ; and the more they think, the more they are. Yet they do not fold their hands in contemplation, rather they fling themselves into life, and their tragedy, if tragedy it can be called, consists in this, that they who by their thought contain life can by no means become a part of that which is but a part of them.

It will be evident that there was no place in this criticism for a detailed account of Dostoevsky's life, though it would be easy, by multiplying quotations from the letters, to elaborate a most pitiful picture of Dostoevsky the man. But the picture would contain only a fragment of the truth. Dostoevsky cannot be understood from his letters ; to understand them

PREFACE

demands first an understanding of his work. Without that, they are obscure; with it, almost superfluous. So is it with his life. There is not a single fact in it that cannot be deduced from his books, and one can with certainty deduce from them infinitely more than the most keen-eyed biographer could discover, or the least reticent dare to tell. All his real life is in his books; he lived in them and for them; they alone contain the anatomy of his tormented soul.

Many of Dostoevsky's minor works have been omitted. To have considered them would have made the work of exposition almost impossible from the point of view which has been deliberately adopted. Many of them were written by Dostoevsky in the intervals between the great novels of his maturity, while he was pondering and shaping the tremendous figures of his imagination. Their composition was at once a distraction and a means of livelihood, for he was always poor. Thus while he was working *Crime and Punishment* in his mind in the years of liberty and poverty which immediately followed his imprisonment, he wrote, besides *The House of the Dead, The Insulted and Injured* and the *Letters from the Under-*

world, all which have a real significance in his evolution, *My Uncle's Dream* and *Stepanchikovo Village*, which have in comparison little or none. They have been left out of account together with many of the immature works of his early years. More questionable may seem the omission of *A Raw Youth* and *The Eternal Husband ;* but they too are relatively of small importance, in the sense that anyone who has followed the gradual evolution of Dostoevsky's greater works, will not hesitate to declare that their writing afforded a brief respite and breathing space from the labour which was peculiarly his own.

The Journal of an Author stands apart. It contains Dostoevsky's reflections upon the events of the day, and above all it contains this political creed. Therein he declares his faith in Russia and prophesies that Russia will obtain Constantinople, because it is written in the book of the destiny of the Russian spirit. In short, Dostoevsky appears in the panoply of a political propagandist. But political propaganda, as it is practised and as Dostoevsky appeared to practise it, was completely foreign to his nature. It is not that he was insincere or that he did not fully mean what he said in the *Journal ;* but the terms which he was forced by circumstances to use were quite inadequate to his intention. His politics were symbolic, and his deliverances upon affairs of the apocalyptic kind. At first sight they read like the leaders of a *bien pensant* newspaper ; but they have an inward meaning of their own. So, when Dostoevsky says that Constantinople must belong to Russia, it is no use for an English politician to reply that it is impossible because of our interests in Egypt and the Eastern Mediterranean. They are not speaking *in pari materia.* Dostoevsky was thinking of the spiritual destiny of the Russian nation. Constantinople will be theirs, he said, without violence. And every Englishman who comprehends Dostoevsky's intention must agree, for in the day when Russia has grown fit to have and to hold her true capital in the manner and the spirit which Dostoevsky foresaw, Englishmen will be no longer talking of interests and empire. Dostoevsky's politics belong to the ideal world, to the future which must be, and therefore already is, of which Prince Myshkin in *The Idiot* said that the Russians did not yet know they were the inheritors.

FYODOR DOSTOEVSKY

Reveal to the Russian the world of Russia, let him find the gold, the treasure hidden from him in the earth ! Show him the whole of humanity, rising again and renewed by Russian thought alone, perhaps by the Russian God of Christ, and you will see into what a wise and truthful giant he will grow, before the eyes of the astounded world, astounded and dismayed, because it expects of us nothing but the sword, nothing but the sword and violence, because judging by themselves, the other peoples cannot picture us free from barbarism. . . .

The Russian thought which shall renew humanity found its most perfect expression in Dostoevsky's novels. In them its development can be seen, and its power felt ; but until it is understood it would be impossible to explain the underlying force of Dostoevsky's political speculations, and when it is understood, unnecessary. Therefore *The Journal of an Author* has only been used in so far as it occasionally serves to make clear the conception of the novels.

The majority of the quotations are taken from Mrs. Garnett's remarkable translations, and I have to thank Mr. William Heinemann for permission to use them. How great an influence Dostoevsky is destined to have upon English

PREFACE

thought and literature no one can prophesy ; but that it will be great and beneficent no one can question. The next generation will be readier than this to recognise the debt that England owes to the translating skill of Mrs. Garnett. For the rest, use has been made of the translation of *Letters from the Underworld* by Mr. C. J. Hogarth in the Everyman Library, and of Miss Colburn Mayne's translation of the German edition of Dostoevsky's Letters, which has been occasionally adapted when the French version seemed to be nearer to Dostoevsky's meaning. The quotations from *The Journal of an Author* are taken from the French translation. In every case when italics are used in these quotations, they are Dostoevsky's own.

J. M. M.

BIOGRAPHICAL NOTE

*Fyodor Mihailovitch Dostoevsky was born on the
30th of October, 1821, in the lodge of the Workhouse
Hospital in Moscow. His father was a doctor on the
staff of the hospital; but it is fairly certain that in
spite of the appearance of soundness and security in his
official position, he and his family were in straitened
circumstances. At the age of sixteen Dostoevsky was
admitted as a cadet into the School of Engineering,
where he remained until 1843. His mother died in
1837 and his father two years later. Before he left the
school Dostoevsky had decided to devote himself to a
literary career. Accordingly in 1844 he resigned the
commission which he had automatically obtained in the
Engineers, and in the following year finished his first
novel, " Poor Folk," and made the acquaintance of the
foremost littérateurs in Petersburg. During the next
three years he worked hard and spent extravagantly.
In 1849 he was arrested together with the other members
of a circle which met in the rooms of one Petrachevsky
to discuss, in a spirit by far more liberal than revolu-
tionary, social and political questions. He was accused
chiefly of having read aloud a famous letter written to*

FYODOR DOSTOEVSKY

Gogol by the critic Bielinsky, and with having taken part in conversations denouncing the severity of the censorship. The sentence of death was passed upon him, but while he was waiting his turn to be shot in the Semyonovsky Square a reprieve arrived commuting his sentence to one of hard labour in Siberia.

He spent four years with the lowest criminals under a régime of terrible severity in the Siberian prison. Though his sentence was completed in February, 1854, it was not until 1859 that he was allowed to return to Petersburg. The next years were chiefly occupied with exacting labour on two magazines which he founded in collaboration with his brother, Mihail. The first, the " Vremia," met with unexampled success until it was suppressed by the administrative stupidity of the Government, for an article on Polish affairs, which the censors could not understand. In the effort to continue the review under the new name of the " Epoca," his brother incurred heavy debts, which, at his death in 1864, Fyodor Dostoevsky took over. In 1866 Dostoevsky remained in Petersburg harassed by creditors, exhausted by illness, writing " Crime and Punishment " ; and to extricate himself from his difficulties he sold the right of publishing his collected works to a thievish publisher for an inadequate sum. He was forced to leave Russia in 1867 to escape imprisonment for debt. While in exile and in extreme poverty he wrote " The Idiot " and " The Possessed." He was unable to return until 1871, when he finally settled in Petersburg. He

BIOGRAPHICAL NOTE

*soon began to publish " The Journal of an Author,"
which appeared periodically, with great success. In
1878 he began to write " The Brothers Karamazov," of
which he only finished the first part. In 1880 he made
the speech upon Pushkin, which was the zenith of his
fame during his own life-time. He was now universally
recognised as one of the greatest Russian writers.*

*In January, 1881, Dostoevsky suddenly ruptured
an artery in his lung. He died within ten days, on the
28th of January, 1881. His funeral was the occasion for
a spontaneous outburst of popular devotion. Melchior
de Vogüé, who was an eyewitness of the ceremony,
wrote of it : " As was said of the old Tsars that they
gathered together the Russian soil, so this king of spirits
had that day gathered together the Russian Heart."*

CONTENTS

		PAGE
	PREFACE	V
	BIOGRAPHICAL NOTE	XV
CHAPTER		
I.	INTRODUCTORY	21
II.	HIS LIFE AND LETTERS	50
III.	THE UNDERWORLD	81
IV.	CRIME AND PUNISHMENT	102
V.	THE IDIOT	129
VI.	THE POSSESSED	157
VII.	THE BROTHERS KARAMAZOV	203
	EPILOGUE	260

I

INTRODUCTORY

DURING the last few years England, or that part of England which reads and thinks, has been confronted in the works of Fyodor Dostoevsky by a new experience. It was inevitable that this new experience should be interpreted by the old and that it should have been made to approximate to familiar standards. The possibility of a new form and a new consciousness cannot be lightly contemplated by any mind : the creation of a new thing, we have neen warned by the most modern philosophy, partakes of the nature of a miracle, and miracles are not easily tolerated in a world of settled convictions. The world of criticism, be it never so liberal, is such a world. It judges by the old, as indeed it must. It seeks to assimilate the present to the past; and it permits of differences in degree only upon the basis of a fundamental identity. A new work of literature is appraised as in some sort a mechanical development from the old : the old units must be recognised before a judgment on the new combination can be passed. This is a safe and right procedure. After all, the creation of a new thing in literature or art is of rare occurrence. We are accustomed to minor creations, and we allow them readily enough. Within the large field of consciousness whose outlying frontiers and general shape we know it is certain that discoveries must continually be made. We have circumnavigated the continent : we have left blank spaces on our map for future explorers : but we are confident that our own firm outline will not be altered. We shall have more knowledge, much more knowledge, if the explorers are brave and unremitting, but it will be knowledge for which we have cupboard-room ; it will not be knowledge of another kind than our own. We do not, and we cannot, furnish for miracles.

And if the miracle were to be brought forth, how should we conduct ourselves towards it ? Certainly we should not recognise it instantly. For instant recognition the mind needs to be prepared, and to be prepared for the miracle of a new thing is already to have created it. We should task ourselves to represent it as a natural and by no means wholly unexpected development of that which we knew before. We should look for the old characteristics and find them, in a different guise perhaps, but in a tolerable likeness which would allow us to see in the apparent difference only a difference of degree. If the matter should happen to be psychology, we should say that the new psychology went deeper than the old, and had brought to light some new facts for whose discovery we had allowed. If the matter were the representation in narrative fiction of human life, we should represent the new creation as the addition to our gallery of portraits of some figures hitherto unobserved, for which, being provident and liberal-minded, we had wall-space and frames in readiness.

Indeed, criticism lives by such occupations. It allots the space, hangs the pictures, affixes a label and makes an entry in the catalogue. After all, pictures are pictures. They do not change in the night and take on some other incalculable being. Years may pass, the hanging need to be changed and the catalogue to be rewritten ; but the pictures are the same : only our knowledge and our tastes have changed. So do books remain books and novels, novels. Our greater and more absorbed attention to them brings us more knowledge, but does not change their nature. Roughly we know the forms of that nature, and we are justified in pointing out for eyes of less dis-

crimination than our own how these forms
recur in the modern productions of the art.
If they are more excellently or more abund-
antly displayed, if like the beneficent railway
itself they have been pushed forward into a
jungle of human experience which knew them
not, then is the praise of criticism their portion.

So English criticism has generously praised
Dostoevsky. It is pleasant to have discovered
a writer of novels who can comfortably be
called great, and to be precise as to the manner
of his greatness. He is a novelist—for did he
not write novels?—of deeper psychological
penetration than his predecessors, who in the
light of his intuition and sympathy has gone
boldly into dark and undiscovered countries
and brought back the results of his explorations.
His form is the same as that his predecessors
used, the novel; his purpose is the same as
theirs, to represent life. Certain of their excellences he has in a much higher degree than
they : certain of their excellences he has not
at all.

With the exception of the last phrase, this
has been the general pattern upon which our
criticism of the work of Dostoevsky has been
built, since his great works began to appear
in English three years ago. He has been made
to conform to the tradition of the art with

which his life was occupied. He has been
allowed a greater measure of subtlety, of penetration, of insight or of sympathy than his for-
bears ; but in the very manner of his praise he
has been safely assimilated to the company of
the elect. And indeed perhaps Dostoevsky
does need, before all things, to be kept fast in
safe company ; but he must be kept there by
the main force of critical complacency. For
the novels of this great novelist have in them
explosive force enough to shatter the very
definition of the novel.

It may be said that there is no such definition, and that each great novelist creates his
own, and is to be judged after the fact. If
this be so, and it is profoundly true, then
Dostoevsky must be so judged. But to judge a
novelist is to compare him with other novelists,
and comparison to be valid and fruitful demands a common element in them all, even
though this common element cannot be described with the exactness of a definition. The
common ground of novelists is a commonplace
of criticism. A novel, in the largest sense of
the word, *represents* life. Life is a process,
whose infinite variety cannot be staled ; it is
a movement in time. Therefore a representation of life must, like its exemplar, be
permeated with this sense of process and

movement ; in the pregnant phrase of a French novelist, it must be, as it were, *baigné dans la durée*, bathed in a sense of time. It must be enveloped in that air in which our physical bodies are born and are nourished, come to maturity and pass on to death. Lacking this atmosphere, the men and women which the novelist creates must inevitably languish and die. Within it they may be as various as is life itself ; to the infinite differences of their physical bodies is added the inexhaustible variety of the human consciousness. But this consciousness depends upon the being of the physical body, and the being of the physical body can be represented only as a process in time. This is the essential condition upon which life may be represented. Where the sense of time is, the sense of growth and process, there is life. Probability and truth in the novelist's art depends pre-eminently upon this.

Whether by deliberate purpose or by unconscious instinct, Dostoevsky set himself in his works to annihilate this sense of time. When we first come into contact with his novels, we are bewildered and grope about in darkness for this clue to reality. We read on as in a dream, and we are in a dream. We read one half *The Idiot*, one half even of *The Brothers Karamazov*, and in reading pass through a fire of spiritual experiences such as one hundred years could not have kindled—and we find that in the measurement of earthly time, but a day has been reckoned. Days such as these are like those of the prophet Daniel, or the Apocalypse, wherein we were taught at school that " times " was a better rendering of the Greek text than " days." " Times, a time and half a time," is assuredly a truer statement of the chronology of Dostoevsky's books than the three and a half days of human measurement. The human measurement had indeed to be marked, for Dostoevsky at least professed to be writing novels ; but the correspondence of the physical day and its spiritual content is fantastic and unreal. It is no wonder that Dostoevsky made grotesque blunders in his registration of this earthly time. At the best his hours are impossible, and it is no great aggravation of his offence that he on occasions flatly contradicts his own calculations. In *Crime and Punishment* Raskolnikov, having decided to confess his crime while he talked with Sonia in the darkness of the night, delays for some sixty pages, and yet finds the office still open, and the sun not yet set when he finally delivers himself up. These things are of no importance, for Dostoevsky is immune from the discipline of time. There is in his works neither night nor day; the sun neither rises nor sets.

Therefore Dostoevsky's novels are not novels at all. They have not that element in their being upon which the novel itself depends. It may of course be said that since they too must be judged after the fact, they merely prove that the sense of time is not after all necessary to the novelist. But if this be accepted, then the novel is not a form of art at all, but only a convenient name for a number of printed pages of prose sold at a price agreed upon by the booksellers. For if a sense of time is not essential to a novel, then a novel is not a representation of life; and if a novel is not a representation of life, what is it? There is surely no larger or more liberal definition of a novel than this, and if this definition is too narrow for the reality, then the reality is indefinable, and all we have gained by our resolute attempts to retain Dostoevsky as an orthodox novelist is the final reduction of the conception of a novelist to an absurdity. But it is foolish to attempt to retain Dostoevsky as a novelist; for it can only be done by failing to recognise him for what he is.

Dostoevsky is not a novelist. What he is is more difficult to define. This book is in the main no more than an attempt towards a

INTRODUCTORY

definition of his essential quality, as this introductory chapter is an attempt to explain the necessity of adopting a new attitude towards his work. A new creation demands a new criticism for its understanding. Our old methods and standards are useless to elucidate and to measure Dostoevsky, not because he is greater than the heroes of art who went before him, but because he is profoundly different. The annihilation of the sense of time in his work is perhaps the most obvious mark of his difference and his fundamental newness. Dmitri Merejhkovsky in his illuminating chapters upon Dostoevsky lets drop the significant hint that Dostoevsky's arbitrary behaviour towards the realities of physical time represents a return to the old unities of the drama, and that Dostoevsky's use of the novel form was due to the constraint of the times in which he lived. This last is probably true in fact; but the return to the unities of drama can only be accepted in a symbolic sense. The very phrase suggests a reaction towards the forms of the past; whereas Dostoevsky's rejection of time is an evidence of his newness. No drama that we know has room prepared for such portentous soliloquies as those of Dostoevsky's heroes. He may indeed have been nearer in spirit to the drama than to the novel; but his drama is a new drama, and one for which the old can stand only as a vague symbol.

Moreover, this absence of a sense of time is relative and not absolute. Physical and actual events take place in Dostoevsky's novels. In reading them we are confounded not so much by the absence of time, as by a continual confusion between what may be called " the timeless world " and the world in time. We are carried from one to the other ruthlessly, and our minds are at the first involved in chaos. We can do no more than to watch the swift unrolling of the incessant vision, and we are fascinated by the mere succession of phantasmagoria. The men and women that we know are inextricably mingled with men and women that we know not, and the known takes from its contact with the unknown a touch of grotesqueness which is bewildering, until in a kind of divine despair we ask ourselves where can this Bohemia be in which the reality partakes so much of the stuff of dreams. The proportion of life, the sweet reasonableness of things human has been dissolved away. Outward acts seem to have been wrenched from their own sequence and to make mock of their familiar logic. Causes are monstrously inadequate to their effects, and the smallest actions of every day take on the character of portents. And yet we know we are not in any kingdom of misrule and madness. We cannot discern the new logic, but a sure instinct tells us that it exists to be discovered. It is rather as though we had been granted a glimpse of the tremendous rites of some secret Brotherhood to which we are not initiate. We discern a significance which we cannot understand, lacking the key and the sign. And so we read on to the end, at moments ascending to the timeless world and again descending to the world where the sun rises, and the flowers spring up and blossom.

Yet a memory as of some unsolved mystery hangs about us, compelling our return. We read again, and some of the dark places are made plain by a new light. Gradually upon the chaos of this pandemonium, with its ecstatic visions of unearthly beauty, simplicity descends. The new proportion, which was concealed from our eyes by the mere succession of the timeless world upon the world in time, is revealed. Some of the figures grow in stature until it seems that no integument of clay can contain the mightiness of their spirit. They pass beyond human comparison, and are no longer to be judged by human laws. That which was evil in our sight, changes swiftly and incessantly, like a point of blinding incan-

descence, from black to white, and white to
black again. Shade appears to be part of the
very essence of light and light of shade, so that
the man who was evil has become a spirit in
whom good and evil are but names for a unity
which contains them both. Those whom we
had thought men and judged and reckoned
upon as men, become as it were transfigured
in our sight : beside them now, the morality
within which we sought so vainly to contain
them is impotent. They burst the bonds of
human law and human time together. Their
earthly acts, their earthly misfortune and
tragedy, even their very names, seem now to
be in some sort a caricature of that which they
are. And as we read, the printed letters of
their names are no longer recognisable ; we
are lost in a wonder that this mean, black hier-
oglyph should contain the awful spirit which
lives within our memory and haunts our imagination.

And while these figures grow, the others
dissolve away. They too are remembered, but
we remember them as living in a world that
has some correspondence with our own. No
longer do they talk and act with the heroes.
Seven circles of the Styx separate them now for
ever. They are in time ; those others have
their being in a world beyond time. Those, we

know, Dostoevsky saw in life; these are the
creatures of his imagination. Those contain
that which he has in common with the novelists
who went before him; these are his own, the
visions which he himself invoked, which have
no counterpart save themselves. They are
awful and mysterious; we see them and we
fear them. In their creation their author
seems to have passed beyond some deep ordinance of human nature, saying, "Thus far
shalt thou go and no further." In the mind
they seek the company of their peers, which
are few and far and hardly understood. That
mocking cruel smile of the "Monna Lisa"
seems to belong to their incarnation, and the
spirits of Dostoevsky and Leonardo to seek
each other across the ages, as those of men who
have sought to pass beyond humanity.

I do not know whether my experience is
common to all those who read and are fascinated by the works of Dostoevsky. There are
times, when thinking about the spirits which
he has conjured up—I use the word deliberately—I am seized by a suprasensual terror.
For one awful moment I seem to see things
with the eye of eternity, and have a vision of
suns grown cold, and hear the echo of voices
calling without sound across the waste and
frozen universe. And those voices take shape

in certain unforgettable fragments of dialogue that have been spoken by one spirit to another in some ugly, mean tavern, set in surrounding darkness, in the pages of Dostoevsky's work. And I am afraid with a fear which chills me even to remember that these spirits should one day put on a mortal body and move among men; and my mind goes back to other moments in my life when this timeless, metaphysical terror has descended upon me. I can ascend slowly, treading firm steps, to the contemplation of eternity and I am not afraid: the slow ascent and the sense that I can as surely descend by the same way I came reassures me. But there have been moments when I have been taken unawares by a sudden *vision* of that which is beyond time, and the timeless world has terribly put on a physical shape. Those moments I cannot forget, and they return to me sometimes when I read and meditate upon Dostoevsky. Because I am convinced that this terror is a part of Dostoevsky's creation, and that he himself was haunted by it even to obsession, I will venture boldly to describe two of these moments in my own experience. They must come to every man who thinks, and to those who understand them they will suggest more quickly than many pages of criticism something of the peculiar and terrible quality of Dostoevsky's work.

The individual terror of these moments consists, I am sure, in the unexpected *physical* presentation of the timeless world. That which can have by its own nature no physical being suddenly, as it were, descends upon some physical object and creates of it a symbol. Perhaps the occasions and the objects will seem ludicrous : indeed they must, for not the least element in their terror is their inadequacy to that which they symbolise. They are a caricature of their own intention.

Once, then, I was reading one of Dr. Wallis Budge's translations of the Egyptian sacred books, and I stumbled upon the phrase " The Boat of the Million Years." I think I should have passed it safely, had it not been that it was repeated several times. Suddenly each faint impression united in my brain and *I saw the boat.* I was cold with horror ; it was as though my very spirit had frozen. I dared not move ; I dared not look out of the window, for I knew that all that lay outside would be old and cold and grey. I remember that I wept bitterly, and sobbed ; the involuntary action seemed to rouse me again to physical life, and the moment was over.

The other occasion was the second time that

FYODOR DOSTOEVSKY

I visited the Zoological Gardens. By chance I stopped before the great cage in which the vultures and condors live. They were perched high up ; their feathers were ragged and grey, and they themselves seemed to be shrinking together as though from cold. Beneath them on the ground was a big, bloody bone. The bone fascinated me ; bits of flesh were clinging to it, and I remember I looked closely at it to see if I could make out what kind of marks their beaks had made upon it. Suddenly I looked up and saw the birds motionless, looking out with blind and lidded eyes. They were set out of time. Though I hated and feared them I could hardly drag myself away. I remember that in a kind of delirium I kept on muttering to myself : " Obscene, obscene," and the word seemed to have taken on a new sense, a profounder meaning. This then, I thought, was the eternal and absolute obscenity. I have thought about it often since, and I think still that there is an obscenity beyond the bodily world, a metaphysical obscenity, which consists in the sudden manifestation of that which is timeless through that which is in time.

This metaphysical obscenity was known to Dostoevsky, it creeps out again and again in his work. The thought of it haunts his great characters, as it haunted himself. It is in a peculiar sense the distinguishing mark of his imaginations. In different forms it recurs continually, either in the thoughts of his characters or in the fates which he devised for them. They are possessed by the horror of it, yet for all their agonised striving to escape it, they are caught by it at the last. For those who are sensible of these things there is more terror and cruelty to Dostoevsky's work than in all the literature of all the ages which went before him. It is not that his is a cruel genius, as men have said, but that he in whom the human consciousness worked more keenly than in other men of his age, was more terribly the victim of the ultimate cruelty of things. He represented that which he saw, and set down his torments in writing. He was obsessed by the *vision* of eternity.

Therefore he could not represent life. For a man who is obsessed by this awful and tremendous vision to represent life is impossible. It is an activity which demands a fundamental acceptance of life. But how should a man whose eyes saw life only too often as something which was cold and dead and infinitely small represent life ? It was to him a mere mockery, and to represent it a barren labour. How could he busy himself with delineating that which at moments he believed did not exist,

in recording words which became suddenly lost
in the silence of eternity? That large acceptance of life which is with the novelist an
instinct was for Dostoevsky something which
he must profoundly question. Faith in life
was what he sought; it was not given to him.
And the motive of his work was not to represent
life, but somehow to justify it.

It would be easy to represent this fundamental character of his work as due to his own
epilepsy, for epilepsy is in itself a means of
bringing the timeless world into sudden contact
with the world in time. But to argue that
Dostoevsky's work was the result of his epilepsy is, besides yielding to the unpardonable
methods of a Nordau, to commit the greater
crime of confounding cause with effect. It is
infinitely more probable that Dostoevsky's
disease, at least in the violent form which it
eventually took, was produced by the incessant
agonies of his mental struggle. His bodily
disease was no more than the concomitant of
his spiritual torments. For, though the characteristic creations of his imagination do for
the most part date from the time at which his
disease entered upon its most violent forms,
they are nevertheless implicit in his work from
its beginnings. There is no sign even in his
earliest writing of that deep acceptance of life

which would have saved him as it saves most
men from the agonies of defying that which is
immutable. His *Poor Folk* reveals him already
as a youth fascinated by the awful fact of Pain.
Never does what he was subsequently (in
A Raw Youth) to call " the living life " appear
in his work ; to him that living life which is
the material of the novelist's art remained either
a miracle in his moments of self-distrust, or in
his moments of belief in his own powers something profoundly ordinary and uninteresting.
And deep down in his philosophy lay the conviction that that which is ordinary is in some
sense unreal. This principle may easily be
deduced from a consideration of his work ;
but since it is stated categorically in one of his
letters, it were best to make use of his own em-
phatic words : —

I have my own idea about art, and it is this : What
most people regard as fantastic and lacking in uni-
versality, *I* hold to be the inmost essence of truth.
Arid observation of everyday trivialities I have long
ceased to regard as realism—it is quite the reverse.
In any newspaper one takes up, one comes across re-
ports of wholly authentic facts which nevertheless
strike one as extraordinary. Our writers regard them
as fantastic, and take no account of them ; and yet
they are the truth for they are facts. . . .

And these everyday trivialities, as he can

call them in the ecstasy of his own creative
fervour—he was then writing *The Idiot*—are
the living life, the life of acceptance—it may
even be called the life of the unconscious.
For Dostoevsky it was not true ; it was something slavish and brute and physical, which,
according to his mood, he either despised or
envied, but did not understand. Not idly did
his Devil in *The Brothers Karamazov* dream of
incarnation irrevocable in the eighteen-stone
wife of a tradesman, to whom the everyday
trivialities should be real and sufficient, and
who in herself despite her proportions was one
of them. But for Dostoevsky only that was
real which was fantastic, in other words, only
that which was the sign of revolt in the mind of
man against the tyranny of life and the iron
laws of blind and cruel nature. For in the
material world and in the dumb and brute
creation the fantastic cannot be : they are
themselves nature. But in the human consciousness which knows itself at once subject
to nature's laws and their master, the fantastic
has already begun. Nay, the mere knowledge
that the mind which knows those laws and is
thereby their master is yet confined within a
tenement of clay which is their slave, is in itself
the very pinnacle of the fantastic, the ultimate
paradox of will, that being will is in itself om-

nipotent, compelled to bow to that which ɪt knows to be its own inferior. The fantastic is the very sign of revolt and protest in man's consciousness against his manifest destiny ; and in this conscious rebellion against life did Dostoevsky find " the inmost essence of the truth " of life.

So in his work, perhaps even in his life, Dostoevsky carried this spirit of conscious rebellion against life to its last extremity. The metaphysical terror with which he was haunted was its most rarefied expression ; as the obsession with that terror is the last agony of the rebellious mind. To conceive, to have the power to conceive, the timeless world, yet physically to be set in the world of time and to be subject to its laws—this is the last verge of the fantastic. There is in this a grotesqueness and obscenity which can freeze the mind which broods upon it with a palsy of horror, which reaches its climax in the sudden vision of the timeless world made apparent in that which is in time. From this contemplation the mind turns away aghast, and Dostoevsky turned away, perhaps to debauch—for there is a quality in his work, the actual poignancy of his suffering in the underworld, which surely could not have attained save at the cost of real experience — certainly to the neurotic dissipation of reckless gambling   Debauch was a protest, gambling was a protest   the frenzy of rebellion was never quiet in his soul   There came the quiet ecstasy of love for his fellow-creatures, who, like him, even though they knew it not, were the victims of the cruelty of a power which he despised. But Dostoevsky's love, even his so-called Christianity, was a revolt. His writing was a frenzy ; his whole life a despairing question.

For though his mind was haunted by the grim terrors of eternity, he knew that he must live. Even though his eyes were drawn incessantly to the sight of Pain, as his mind could not away with the vision of the timeless world, his body was in time. However much and with whatever extreme of passion he denied life, he was part of life. He was more than unwilling part of life, he was a lover of life ; perhaps only those whose minds are driven to the desolation of ineffectual rebellion against life, are its true lovers. They alone see life apart from themselves, and long for it. Other men are life : to be life's lover one must be separate from it. And Dostoevsky was separated from it by a gulf so great that it seems a cruel joke to call him part of life ; and as he was set apart from men by the twofold barrier of his tormented mind and of the disease which was the physical symbol of those

torments, so did he yearn with a double passion
to be among them. He could look upon life,
" the living life," and see that it was good, for
those who could share it without his torments,
without his perpetual brand of bodily imper-
fection. He coveted life ; therefore his own
life was an unending struggle to reconcile himself with life. His fond dream of incarnation
irrevocable in the eighteen-stone wife of a
tradesman was denied him in this existence,
as he knew it must be denied. But he dreamed
another dream. He dreamed that man, the
conscious being, capable of terror beyond the
physical, with the knowledge to know all
things, and the courage to look upon them
without the cowardice of self-delusion, might
pass beyond the condition of protest and rebellion and find a way of life. He dreamed
that there might be a secret hidden from his
conscious seeking, which, when he knew, would
serve him as a key to the mystery ; and in the
triumphant knowledge of that secret his being
would open to the full acceptance of life. And
the name of that secret was in his language,
God, and the name of the knowledge which he
dreamed, Faith. In truth, he was a God-
tormented man. " God has tortured me all
my life," says Kirillov in *The Possessed*. God
was for him the possibility of acceptance, the

hope of a way of life. He knew that belief in
God as a person, the faith of religion as we
understand religion, was denied him for ever.
He asked for no more than a way of life. What
must he *do* to be saved ? The posing of that
terrible problem and the attempt to answer it
with something more than barren silence, forms
the deep argument of his greatest books. In
his letters appears again and again his conception of hero : a man who has lost his faith
and does not dare to be a sceptic. Perhaps it
may sound simple enough, but the implications
of the conception are infinite and tremendous.
Every one of those implications was present
to Dostoevsky's mind. Faith in the sense in
which he desired it was not a matter for plat-
form debate or the cheap denial of secular
societies ; on it hung his very life. Man must
live, and being man must know whereunto he
lives, or he does not live at all. Yet the man
who is most truly man can acquiesce in no
limitations to his knowledge, for to know is to
be man, and to know utterly is to be most
wholly man. He who knows utterly, knows
that there is nothing unto which he lives. He
is not fooled by the easy gospel of the infinite
perfectibility of human nature. Man is among
the things which he knows, and he knows that
man will never be more perfect than he is, un-

less his nature, nay, his very physical body, be changed. No facile gospel of social progress will avail him. Shall he who knows that in himself he contains the extreme perfection of human nature as it is, servilely declare his belief in a future for which his perfection must be sacrificed like a dumb brute at the altar ?

This is no mere dilemma of the schools, for great minds and great men, who demand that nothing shall be hid from them. But to face it asks perhaps more than mortal courage. It must ask more than mortal courage, for there has never been a man who has dared to confront it wholly and for all his life. To have this daring is to pass beyond mortality. Or it may be there have been such men, and their names have perished out of all remembrance, for they must surely die at the hands of their fellow-men. They cannot have this question tormenting their souls, and yet remain the citizens of a city : they must be led without the walls and stoned until they die : for assuredly the spirit of evil lives in them. There is no false step in the awful logic of Ivan Karamazov : If there is no God, then all things are lawful. Dostoevsky was the first writer to make that logic plain. His imagination conceived men who were driven by the force of their own humanity to confront the issue.

However terrible they may appear—and they appear as portentous spirits—it is their humanity which compels them to know all things, and those things above all that some undying instinct tells us must not be known. For they seek a way of life, and that seeking is the very mark of humanity.

Beside these figures the myriad other characters of Dostoevsky's creation fade away. They are no more than the material out of which his own particular creations were fashioned. They are, as it were, the life upon which his great characters have brooded. They are suffering humanity, against whose suffering the giant minds have rebelled not merely in thought, but in act. Therefore they have but a small place in this book, not because they form one indistinguishable mass, for they do not, but because their creation was no more than the prelude to Dostoevsky's own achievement, which was to represent the mind of humanity rebellious against the life in which the suffering of the lesser creatures was inevitable, and with the ultimate courage of rebellion. This is but a part of what he did. His work is the record of a great mind's seeking for a way of life ; it is more than a record of struggle, it is the struggle itself. Dostoevsky sent forth mighty champions to battle with life for its secret, men who dared far more than their mortal lives—the only terror death had for them was their fear of being deceived by their own *beau geste*—men who in the combat dared to *will evil ;* and the battle-ground is his great books. Besides these champions, as in the Homeric struggle of old, the people fell, without number and without name. But in Dostoevsky the people have their names, their individual being that cannot be forgotten ; only the mind which is fastened upon the single combat and the champions cannot hold the lesser folk within its vision. Yet these are drawn as no one before Dostoevsky had drawn them. All that the human soul can suffer is somewhere expressed within his work ; but there are lesser and greater sufferings, or rather there are sufferings and there is absolute suffering. Suffering may be forgotten in happiness ; but absolute suffering never. Dostoevsky's heroes are tormented by this absolute suffering : their minds are never free from the gnawing terror of the timeless world. Therefore they are not human. Man cannot suffer for ever. They are disembodied spirits. They have the likeness of men, we are told, but we know that we shall never look upon them. Nikolay Stavrogin's face was like a mask, says the story of *The Possessed.* They have all faces

like masks, for no physical flesh could bear the
lineaments of those spirits. Their bodies are
but symbols, which may suggest that these are
possibilities of the human spirit, possibilities
which Dostoevsky alone had dared to contemplate.

Therefore it would be useless even to attempt
to consider the superhuman figures of this
symbolic world, and the lesser men and
women of the world we know, together in a
criticism of Dostoevsky's work. The human
figures would be dwarfed in the comparison.
Moreover, even were the method possible, it
would be false. Dostoevsky was not a novelist,
and he cannot be judged as a novelist. His
superhuman and his human figures do not
differ from each other in the degree of their
humanity ; they are absolutely different, and
it is in them that the strangeness and the fascination and the power of Dostoevsky rests.
They are the champions ; the issue of the
battle rests with them. If they can be understood, then the rest of Dostoevsky's literary
creation will fall as though automatically into
its place.

But Dostoevsky's art was gradually evolved
through the forms of the novel. The slow
emergence of his own essential conceptions,
and their evolution to the final vision of *The*

INTRODUCTORY

Brothers Karamazov can be traced through his
books from the beginning, until at the last each
of his great novels seems to mark an epoch in
the human consciousness. In the following
chapters of this book an attempt is made to
follow out this evolution.

II

HIS LIFE AND LETTERS

In the outward and visible life of Dostoevsky are three great facts : his death-sentence, his imprisonment, and his epilepsy. By these his life was set apart from among the lives of other men for the more perfect manifestation of his spirit.

At the age of twenty-seven, he was condemned to death. While he was waiting his turn to be executed, he was reprieved. For a moment he had been suspended on the edge of annihilation or eternity. Without leaving life, without even loosing his hold upon consciousness, he had in that moment passed beyond life. He had been poised open-eyed on the narrow verge which divides life from that which is not life ; he had been lifted out of the living world.

Nor could he descend to it again. His four years in prison in Siberia served only to strengthen and make impassable the barrier that had suddenly been cast between him and

life. In the moment in which he faced death he
had been torn by the roots out of life ; in the
four years of his imprisonment the habit of
separation entered irrevocably into his being.
He endured the severance ; and he grew strong
and proud in his isolation. The bodily man
which holds the timeless soul in time became
hardly more than a fragile shell. It was sub-
ordinated to the spirit which it housed. In
itself it did not weaken ; but its strength was
its own no more. It lived because Dostoevsky's
spirit desired to live. His soul gave his body
nourishment, not his body fed his soul.

And in his epilepsy the last community between these elements was broken. There were
moments now when his spirit left his body and
ascended into another condition of being, and
the last link between Dostoevsky and life was
snapped. He was in life, but he was not of it
any more.

Therefore the three great events of Dostoevsky's outward life are such as make a
mockery of the word " life," if it be applied to
him. Between him and earthly reality was no
genuine contact, and he lived as one to whom
a sense of the practices and possibilities of
ordinary existence had been denied. His
miserable poverty, his utter recklessness with
money, his complete ignorance of earthly

economy whether of his possessions or himself, are not in him mischances to be deplored. They were an essential part of him. He cannot be conceived without them ; they were the necessary condition of his embodiment. For, fantastic as it may sound, Dostoevsky existed more truly as an idea than as a man. He was a consciousness incarnate, and in him the preponderance of the spirit over the body reached the extreme beyond which lay the death of the physical man and the dissolution of the spiritual being.

Therefore it is unprofitable to examine into Dostoevsky's life more closely. It is to a fantastic degree full of suffering and poverty, extravagance and enthusiasm, which according to the general interpretation is a sign of the nervous strain under which he lived. But with far greater truth it may be said that the reason was that life itself was in a profound sense inadequate to him. He could not express himself within its forms at all. He was like a troubled spirit seeking incarnation ; he was a stranger to life and, entering into it, he conducted himself as one who, unlike the rest of men, had not been trained from childhood in its etiquette.

From the first he was rather a mind brooding on life than a living man. It is probable that the nervous disorder which was eventually to develop into the terrible epilepsy which ravaged his later life had a firm hold of his system while he was yet a boy ; as a boy, undoubtedly, he felt that he was set apart from his fellows. Consciousness had already marked him for her own. All the instinctive joys and satisfactions which being the natural expansion of the animal in man, are the solid and unshakable foundations of life, were remote from him. He felt himself no part of the common soul ; and though he longed to lose himself and to be submerged beneath the waters he could not. His consciousness was tyrannical from the beginning, and his whole life may be seen as the constant effort either to be wholly conscious and thus to escape from life or to overthrow the tyranny of his mind and be swallowed up in the flood.

At the very end of his life Dostoevsky wrote to a correspondent that there was " but one cure, one refuge for the woe of living alone and constantly opening the wounds in one's soul : art, creative activity." This was the only way of life for one who only externally formed part of life. Dostoevsky had to live in the world fashioned by the imagination of his conscious mind ; in the real world he was a stranger and an outcast. In that world his only hope of existence lay in the extremity of sensation. He did not indeed choose for himself a sentence of death and a burial in the dead-house of Siberia : those sufferings descended upon him ; and yet it may surely be said that they were inevitable for him. He would, at least, have created their counterpart for himself in life. He who sought the underworld of dissoluteness and debauchery, in the hope that he might find a means of living, had already pronounced his own death-sentence and immured himself in a prison. The actual events of his life were hardly more than the rather crude and material manifestation of the natural working of his own spirit. He was born a prisoner in life, with the sentence of mortal death hanging over him. These things were written in the book of his destiny ; by their actual agency he came to be more perfectly and more quickly that which he by nature was, a man in whom bodily existence was completely subservient to the life of the soul. If, by some miracle, a way had been found by which his spirit could have lived in final divorcement from his body, Dostoevsky would have been driven to that way.

So it is that the outward and visible life of Dostoevsky is in the nature of a clumsy symbol of that which he really was. Never was a man towards whose understanding biography could less contribute. He did not fit into the forms of general life, and he cannot be defined by his relations to them. Looked at from the angle of rational human existence, he is a monstrosity. He had no life : that which served him for life was a long sequence of suffering upon suffering, extreme sensation piled upon extreme sensation. It is one huge grotesque and heart-rending blunder, utterly devoid of beauty, and balance and sanity. It is the manifestation of some great and unknown power in a medium foreign to it, as though, to borrow a geometrical figure, a reality which had four dimensions had been compelled to manifest itself in three. The category of life could not contain Dostoevsky's being which existed in another category ; and this " incommensurability " of Dostoevsky with the forms which were before him is a characteristic which profoundly distinguishes him, not merely from other men, but from other men of genius. His living spirit was incommensurable with the forms of life, his art with the forms of art. He cannot be approached by the same road as other men, and how great is the error of those who make the attempt has been lately shown by the absurdity into which a realistic critic of his life has fallen headlong.

FYODOR DOSTOEVSKY

Let one significant instance be taken—Dostoevsky's letters. They are profoundly interesting, but in a way absolutely different from that in which the letters of other great writers are interesting. Their significance is really negative : they are not letters at all. In them he reveals in the positive sense nothing of himself, and the reader is constantly overwhelmed by the conviction that he cannot express himself by this means at all. They consist of rows of figures, frenzied calculations, heart-rending appeals ; and even upon these matters they are always incoherent. When he makes the endeavour to explain his ideas, or the plan of the work on which he happens to be engaged, he is quite unintelligible. To communicate his thoughts or the experiences of his soul to another person was for him impossible. He realised it himself, and gave up the attempt. It may of course be said that he was continually so oppressed by poverty and overwork, that he had no time for the amenities of correspondence. This could not in any case be a very acceptable solution. Even a Dostoevsky had his moments when he could breathe freely ; and the experience of history is that good writers write good letters. But in any case the last ten years of Dostoevsky's life were comparatively free from anxiety. His position in

the world was secure and even comfortable.
And what do we find him confessing in the last
year of his life, to a correspondent whom he
evidently regarded with affection ? " Forgive
the untidiness of my letter. If you only knew
how I am loving the capacity to write letters
and what a difficulty I find it ! . . ." Here
Dostoevsky bewails the loss of a capacity
which he had never possessed. We need not
confine ourselves to his actual confessions—
though perhaps the only approach to a jest in
all his correspondence is in the words : " If I go
to Hell, I shall certainly be condemned for my
sins to write ten letters a day "—the evidence
of his inability to write a letter is the whole of
the letters which he wrote. One feels almost
that they were written by an illiterate person.
And so in a sense they were, save that Dostoevsky's illiteracy lay, as it were, beyond letter-
writing. For letters are the literary expression
of a common social life. Their excellence depends upon a sense of that community in the
soul of the writer. In a good letter one mind
unbosoms to another in the common language
of their mutual souls. Dostoevsky's letters
have no such intimacy ; they have not even
dignity. There seems to have been nothing in
common between him and his correspondents
save the actual Russian language which he

used, while his share even of this community
seems to have been precarious. When he is not
dealing with the mathematical units of his
money affairs, he appears to be struggling in
vain to express to another something which
can be expressed to himself alone.

His letters can only be understood by a close
study of his books. Without that they are
unintelligible, or rather too easily intelligible,
for he does not say what he means to say. His
expression falls woefully short of his intention
in them, because he is forced to speak in a kind
of symbolic language, of which his imaginative
works are the only dictionary. And in this his
letters make one with his life : or better, if the
relation is not too complicated, they are a
symbol of the outward life which in its turn
was only a symbol of his living spirit. The
same extravagance, the same incoherence, the
same inadequacy, the same incommensurability
and the same consciousness of all these failures
in expression, are to be found both in his
letters and his life. With the same truth he
might have said (as, indeed, if the complex
connection be followed, he actually did say)
at the end of his year : " Forgive the untidiness of my life ! If you only knew how I am
loving the capacity to live, and what a difficulty I find it ! . . ."

HIS LIFE AND LETTERS

Dostoevsky is essentially a consciousness, and his history is to be sought not in his letters or in any biography, but in the evolution of the creative mind which is traced in his books. And they, likewise, cannot be regarded as human histories : life was as inadequate for his imaginations as it was for his own spirit, and his own life can only be read truly as one of his own stories, in which the realistic happenings play but a minor and, in the last resort, an unessential part. Even that portion of his biography which was written by his own hand, the account of his experiences in the Siberian prison in *The House of the Dead*, is of small account in his work. It belongs, like his letters, to his external history, and, for all its great interest, might have been written by another man. Or it may be considered as the most lucid and the longest of Dostoevsky's letters ; and it is no more. Of what he really suffered there and really thought it contains hardly a hint, and we can gather infinitely more knowledge of his inward life during that time of entombment from one casual sentence in his letters than from the whole of his narrative. That casual sentence tells us that in prison he thought out *Crime and Punishment*. To understand his life in prison an understanding of that book is necessary ; for, compared with *Crime and Punishment, The House of the Dead* is an accomplished exercise in the better kind of journalism, which sets itself the imparting of new information as its ideal. *The House of the Dead* is full of fascinating information; but when one has lived long with Dostoevsky's work, such information is trivial and of no account. A new thirst rises within one, the thirst for a fuller knowledge of Dostoevsky's soul, and this can by no means be satisfied by *The House of the Dead.*

The House of the Dead is the record of an episode in his actual life which has no place in the sequence of his spiritual experience. Yet considered not for itself but as the outward semblance of a period of intense inward life the book may serve as a landmark. But, regarded from this point of view, it is significant only for that which it deliberately omits; its professed object is to give " a vivid and concrete picture of prison life in the second division and all that I have lived through in those years." The last phrase must be a grim joke, for Dostoevsky thus continues : —

I remember that all that time, though I had hundreds of companions, I was fearfully lonely, and at last I grew fond of that loneliness. In my spiritual solitude I reviewed all my past life, went over it all to the smallest detail, brooded over my past, judged myself sternly and relentlessly, and even sometimes blessed fate for sending me this solitude, without which I could not have judged myself like this, nor have reviewed my past life so sternly. And what hopes set my heart throbbing in those days! I believed, I resolved, I swore to myself that in my future life there should be none of the mistakes and lapses there had been in the past. I sketched out a programme for myself for the whole future, and I firmly resolved to keep to it. The blind faith that I should and could keep these resolutions rose up in my heart again. I looked forward eagerly to freedom, I prayed for it to come quickly ; I longed to test myself in fresh strife. At times I was overcome by nervous impatience. But it hurts me now to recall my spiritual condition at that time. Of course all that concerns no one but me. . . .

All that concerned no one but him—and he had professed to give an account of all that he lived through during those years !

But we know something of what he did live through, for we know that in prison he conceived, if not Svidrigailov, at least Raskolnikov ; and we can gather up the evidence that is broadcast over his later work. We have also the testimony of his earlier work, and we can imagine without much fear of deception what manner of mind was Dostoevsky's when he entered The House of the Dead, and what change was wrought in him by four years' incessant brooding over human destiny. We

have, too, the letters which he wrote to those
he thought might understand a little, if only a
little, more than the readers for whom he com-
posed *The House of the Dead*.

Dostoevsky's first novel, *Poor Folk*, will
serve as typical of all that he wrote before the
convulsion in his inward life which was mir-
rored to the world in his death-sentence and
his imprisonment. He wrote much besides in
this period, but his other works are of inferior
merit in the same kind. *Goliadkin*, for instance, has a touch of the fantastic in its narra-
tion of the adventures of a poor official with
his *alter ego*, and *The Lady of the House* is
mysterious to the point of being unintelligible;
but neither of them contains any evidence that
Dostoevsky had passed beyond the ideas and
sensibility which were the basis of *Poor Folk*.
He was still sheltered beneath Gogol's *Cloak*.
Gogol's comedy and Gogol's sympathy were
his inspiration, and his poor official, Dievushkin, was derived more or less directly from his
master.

But Dostoevsky used Gogol's manner as
one born to it. He was born to it. The infinite
tenderness with which the simple, self-sacri-
ficing love of Dievushkin for Barbara is de-
picted was his own and was to remain his for
ever. The hopeless tragedy of the story reveals

him already looking with open eyes upon the pain and suffering that are in the world. He makes no attempt to compromise with them. There is no hope for Dievushkin and none for Barbara. She is forced by her poverty to marry the coarse and unfeeling man who seduced her, and he is left alone in Petersburg with nothing but a memory of what might have been in another world to comfort him. Nor is there any heroism : Dievushkin's grandiloquence and his preoccupation with his own style are ridiculous. He is timid and terrified of the rumour of " free-thought " in his reflections. He is even resigned to his lot, and he would never contemplate rebellion against the power which has thus condemned him, even in a dream. He could never be anything greater than a kind, happy and generous man ; and this he could so easily be that his suffering is not tragic, but merely painful. And the whole book is like one long sob of pain, inflicted by a senseless power which had not the wit to choose a worthier antagonist to crush.

To describe *Poor Folk* at length would be to give it undue importance. It is the book of a boy ; but the boy was Dostoevsky. Its unflinching honesty and tender sympathy are very beautiful ; but its significance is rather historic than permanent. Romanticism was still flourishing when Dostoevsky was a youth, and the strange phantasmagoria of *The Lady of the House* shows that he himself was influenced by its more sombre manifestations. But in *Poor Folk* he declares himself realist through and through ; he is preoccupied with life and not with dreams, as though by instinct he had been warned that the only dreams of substance are those which come after the soul has been steeped in the common reality. He turned himself immediately towards the fact of pain, and did not lower his eyes, neither did he deceive himself with consolations, for the suffering in *Poor Folk* is not the suffering which is supposed to make men, but that which prevents men from being men. A Barbara is degraded and brutalised by her pain ; her senses are so numbed that she herself in the end becomes unfeeling. Dostoevsky is too easily supposed to have preached a gospel of " purification by suffering." That is a comfortable doctrine, invented by those who have not suffered, to enable them to look calmly upon others' pain ; but Dostoevsky did not hold it. In *Poor Folk*, his first utterance concerning the life he saw and felt, he showed that he could never hold it. What need had a Makar Dievushkin or a Barbara Dobroselova of purification, and how were they purified ?

The pain which they suffered was justified neither in itself nor in them ; under its fictitious alchemy, they did not become heroes nor were their small destinies raised to the heights of tragedy. They had the satisfaction neither of accepting nor denying the evil which oppressed them ; they were merely stunned and bewildered by it.

But, though they did not rebel, Dostoevsky himself did. The mere fact that he could so present them, tormented to no end, is the evidence of a protesting mind. We have the letters to show what form the protest took in Dostoevsky's early manhood. " My health is already shattered," he wrote to his brother when he had finished *Goliadkin*, " I am neurotic and dead low fever. I am so dissolute that I simply can't live decently any more. . . ." An unflinching knowledge of the fact of pain in the world is a dangerous burden for a young man's soul to bear. Dostoevsky rebelled against it, but he had not yet attained the calm and the strength to devise a form for his rebellion ; he had not yet the force to build up a tower in his own soul where he could abide apart from the life to which he would not admit his vassalage. He had not learned how to live to himself, though he had learned the necessity. Dostoevsky had a clear insight into the nature of his malady. " It is indeed true," he wrote to his brother when he was twenty-six, " that the dissonance and lack of equilibrium between ourselves and society is a terrible thing. External and internal things should be in equilibrium. For, lacking external experiences, those of the inward life will gain the upper hand, and that is most dangerous. . . ." Most dangerous indeed, and yet that dangerous road was marked out for Dostoevsky at his birth. There is no equilibrium possible between the rebellious soul and the life against which it does rebel, and Dostoevsky, so keenly scenting the danger, could only make desperate efforts to redress the balance by flinging himself, as it were, bodily into the scale of life. To fling one's self into life for the sake of poising the torments of consciousness with the sensations of eternal experience is a remedy worse perhaps than the disease ; but it was one with which Dostoevsky could not long have deceived himself. The equilibrium that had once been disturbed could never be recovered this side eternity : dissipation of whatever kind would never right the scale. Dostoevsky forgot nothing of his youth in his age. " I'm sorry you call that rebellion," Ivan Karamazov was eventually to say, " One can't live in rebellion, and I want to live." But in those days Dosto-

evsky had still to learn that it was of no use to
want to live ; he had to learn to accept his
destiny, and to work out his own salvation, not
in harmony with life, but in grim and complete
rebellion against it.

Upon the youthful chaos of rebellion against
life and rebellion against rebellion, of consciousness of equilibrium lost and vain attempts
consciously to restore the harmony, of protest
against life and the overwhelming desire to
live, fell the death sentence and Siberia, like
the sudden blow which sets a disordered heap
of little sand into a pattern. Now there was
no room for the despairing effort after harmony,
nor any opening for the frenzied plunge into
life. Dostoevsky could sit alone for four
terrible years with his bitter knowledge for sole
companion, and think and think and think.
. . . No wonder he set his lips to silence when
he wrote *The House of the Dead*. I have for
myself only one vision of Dostoevsky in the
body. Sometimes I see him walking up and
down in the space behind the sheds of the
prison yard, clothed in convict motley, one leg
black, the other grey, the colour of his coat
likewise divided, his head half-shaved and
bent forward, thinking, thinking . . . and I am
frightened of those thoughts.

But the years passed. Dostoevsky, who

entered the prison a youth, emerged a man.
As the sardonic phrase runs—although those
who use it seem to be wholly innocent of sardonic intent—he had been " purified by suffering." He had entered a lion, and he came out
a lamb—a Christian, a patriot, a citizen, a
social being. It is wonderful what a little un-
just imprisonment, what four years' hell on
earth could do for the most sensitive soul that
modern civilisation has brought forth. Such
faith in the moral governance of modern
society is too sublime to be shaken. People
who will believe that Dostoevsky was purified
by his suffering or that he believed in such
purification, will believe anything. They will
believe that Dostoevsky was a Slavophil or
that he believed in the Christian God. They
will believe what it is comfortable for them to
believe. Therefore they will not believe in the
real Dostoevsky. He is not at all comfortable.

The rest of this book is devoted to tracing
out what manner of thoughts they really were
that Dostoevsky laboured in his mind during
the long silence and suffering of his imprisonment. They cannot be anticipated here, for
they grew gradually as they were incessantly
shaped under the intense pressure of Dostoevsky's creative imagination until his death.
The labour of his life henceforward was to

translate the deep thoughts of his mind into imaginative terms ; he had to create symbols which should express ideas of the most transcendental kind. Those things which had become a bitter and terrible reality to him, he had to make real to other minds than his own. He had to do more than this : he had to test his thought in the crucible of an imagined world. I do not think that Dostoevsky, even when his mind was most warmly kindled by the enthusiasm of hope, dreamed that he would be wholly comprehended by his contemporaries : from the form of his great works alone, wherein he sets his heroes among a multitude of men who do not understand them, it is certain that he did not. He worked for himself, trying his own thoughts as by fire, and for the future.

For there is no writer of any age or any country in whom abstract thought has lit so mighty a flame of passion as in Dostoevsky. In him the most terrible and the most human of all passions, the passion to know, reached to the heat of incandescence. Abstract thought was for him not merely a fascinating occupation, as it is with many philosophers so called, not a habit of mind learned in a school, but an awful necessity upon which his life depended. It was born anew in him from the shock of his

contact with life itself. All his life long the eye
of his soul was turned to the contemplation of
Pain. As a boy, he had looked upon it bravely ;
his final words, spoken as a dying man, were
directly inspired by this life-long contemplation. All the questions which all philosophy
has asked when fronted with this reality were
gathered up in him : he went beyond the
searchings of philosophy. He dared to ask
more than the philosophers ; he dared to ask
in another way ; he dared to believe that man
must have the courage of his humanity, to put
faith in the sovereignty of his own mind, and
to make his metaphysic the bitter bread of his
actual life.

These things cannot yet be made plain ; nor
can it be made wholly plain that the years of
prison life were those in which Dostoevsky
came to the knowledge of his determination
and his genius. He would have come to that
knowledge without an occasion so terrible we
cannot doubt ; the years in the wilderness were
for such a spirit inevitable. But Destiny con-
spired to make those years actual. People will
not easily believe that a man can suffer in his
soul ; but they will believe in four years' imprisonment. That is a fact which is convincing, and so perhaps *The House of the Dead*
had its purpose. " There is suffering and suffer-

ing," says Ivan Karamazov, " degrading
humiliating suffering such as humbles me—
hunger, for instance—my benefactor will perhaps allow me ; but when you come to higher
suffering—for an idea, for instance—he will
very rarely admit that, perhaps because my
face strikes him as not at all what he fancies a
man should have who suffers for an idea."
Dostoevsky needed the reputation of a convict
condemned in order that people should believe
in him. But if this knowledge has made them
listen to him, it has not helped them to understand him. " There is suffering and suffering," to know that is to know the key to
Dostoevsky. The gulf between these two is so
great that the one which is outward and visible
may be a heaven of refuge from the other ; and
the danger of recognising the obvious torment
of Dostoevsky's life in prison, which he himself described, is that it may draw men's attention from the other suffering which made
him what he was.

Dostoevsky himself confided these sufferings,
to no one. In *The House of the Dead*, he deliberately held his peace. Perhaps he did not
dare to speak ; he had to wait his hour, when
he should have found a means of expressing
himself in the language of the imagination,
which to many will always seem obscure and

71

impersonal. He might safely count upon it that the world would not recognise him for what he was, or his art and his heroes for what they were, until long after he was dead. And, indeed, he was perfectly safe : even now it seems barely to be understood that he created heroes of a different kind from any that had been before. Hamlet and Faust alone stretch out a hand to them. They are heroes not of action, or of life, but of thought. They think terribly, and have the courage of their thinking : though they dare to act, it is not their action that matters, but their thought alone. This one characteristic of Dostoevsky's figures is enough to divide them absolutely from their ancestors. But what is still more significant is that their creator is by them absolutely divided from his predecessors. To imagine a man in act, and to imagine a mind in act, are two utterly different things. A mind in act, if it shall be convincing, must be presented as a perfect mind. There is no room for a flaw in logic. A man who acts from a mistaken idea is after all a man. It is his act which matters, not his mind. But a hero of thought must be immune from such weakness. His reasoning must be unanswerable, if not to all men, at least to the mind which conceived him. Thought is the very blood within the veins of

such an incarnation ; if it runs thin or is
corrupt the imagination languishes and dies.
Which is to say that Dostoevsky himself
thought the thoughts of his thinking heroes :
he lavished his own blood to make them live.
*He created them because the reasoning which
they embodied was to him unanswerable.* That
was the indispensable condition of their
being.

No wonder, then, that he did not dare to
speak, when he came out from prison, into the
light of day after four years thinking alone.
We have the letter he wrote to his brother
then, which is the most meaning of all his
letters, because the silence which pervades
them all is here most full of meaning.

I won't even try to tell you what transformations
were undergone by my soul, my faith, my mind and
my heart in those four years. It would be a long
story. Still, the eternal concentration, the escape
into myself from bitter reality, did bear its fruit. I
now have many new needs and hopes of which I never
thought in other days. But all this will be a pure
enigma for you, so I'll pass to other things. . . .

And yet it would have been so simple to give
one half a page to an outline of the new gospel
of salvation by suffering : that would not have
been difficult to explain, nor an enigma when

explained. He might have told his brother of
the joys of brotherly Christian love, which he
is supposed to have discovered in the prison
barrack. He might at least have told of the
promise he is supposed to have found in the
simple hearts of the Russian peasant criminals, whose society he had so long enjoyed.

Yet he did none of these things. He was
strangely recalcitrant. As for the simple
hearts, he said : " I dread simple men more
than complex men " ; as for brotherly love,
he calls his fellow-convicts " rough, angry and
embittered men " ; and as for his own salvation by suffering, he confesses, " My own
character was deteriorating ; in my relations
with others I was ill-tempered and impatient."
Perhaps the new needs and hopes were not so
simple after all. The one great need which he
declares to his brother is the need of books.
And what books ? " Modern historians : Gui-
zot, Thierry, Thiers, Ranke and so forth ;
national studies and Fathers of the Church."
That was solid food enough to satisfy the most
imperious hunger ; but it was not the food he
craved. " Send me," he writes later on in the
letter, " the Koran and Kant's *Critique of Pure
Reason*, and if you have the chance of sending
anything *not* officially, then be sure to send me
Hegel—but particularly Hegel's *History of*

Philosophy. My whole future depends upon that. . . ."

Has any other man ever written that his whole future depended upon his receiving Hegel ? Hegel, Kant's *Critique,* and a German dictionary—these were the outward needs. It was hardly strange that he should have thought that the inner longings which they might satisfy would be an enigma to his brother. His needs had passed to the transcendental ether now, and it was but natural that his hopes should be set in the same distant heaven. He had begun to ask great questions and to turn, surely with a premonition of despair, to the great philosophers for an answer. Upon them his whole future depended. So Dostoevsky may for the moment have thought. But what philosopher could answer his metaphysical doubts ? He would find them barren and be forced to know that his whole future depended upon himself alone.

But it is not likely that he was buoyed with such a hope. The mind which had begun to conceive *Crime and Punishment* had little enough to expect from the *Critique of Pure Reason* or the *Phenomenology of Spirit.* What Kant and Hegel had thought out in the categories of abstract reason, Dostoevsky was to create anew, by the force of his own spirit, in

the category of flesh and blood ; and he was
to go beyond them. His life's work had begun
to take shape in the depths of his mind. " I
planned out a great novel," he says in another
letter written at about the same time to Maikov, " which I consider will be my definitive
work. I was dreadfully afraid that the first
passion for my work would have grown cold
when the years had passed, and the hour of
realisation struck beyond recall. But I was
mistaken : the figure which I had conceived
and which is the basis of the whole book
needed some years for its development, and
I am convinced that I should have ruined all
if I had then, unready as I was, begun the work
in the first flush of zeal. . . ." And in the same
letter he writes again : " When one's young,
ideas come crowding incredibly into one's
head, but one should not capture each and all
of them as it flies and rush to give it forth.
One should rather await the synthesis, and
think more ; wait till the many single details
which make up an idea have gathered themselves into a nucleus, into a large imposing
picture : then and not till then should one
write them down. The colossal figures created
by the colossal writers have often grown out
of long stubborn labour. . . ."

Metaphysical anguish born of long brooding

upon the reality of pain, the long stubborn
labour of thinking all the thoughts of Raskolnikov, with even then the more terrible thought
of Svidrigailov lurking in the recesses of his
mind—these were hardly the exercises to which
a soul in process of being purified by suffering
would be given during the time of purification,
or a mind which was being painfully regenerated
by the Christian verities. Dostoevsky would
have given much to have had the relief of faith
in them, but he would not have been Dostoevsky had he found it. How could he find repose in the consolations of religion, whose
" Hosanna had been thus tried in the crucible
of doubt " ? But there is a third letter written
at the same time which, without concealment,
declares his true attitude to Christianity.
Moreover, it serves to complete this outline of
Dostoevsky's spiritual condition when he had
passed the grand climacteric of his inward,
and only, life.

I want to say to you about myself, that I am a
child of this age, a child of unbelief and scepticism,
and probably—indeed I know it—shall remain so
until the end of my life. How terribly it has tortured
me (and tortures me even now)—this longing for
faith, which is all the stronger for the proofs I have
against it ! And yet God gives me sometimes moments of perfect peace ; in such moments I love and

believe that I am loved ; in such moments I have formulated my creed wherein all is dear and holy to me·
This creed is extremely simple : here it is : I believe
that there is nothing lovelier, deeper, more sympathetic, more rational, more human and more perfect
than the Saviour ; I say to myself that not only is
there no one else like Him, but that there could be no
one. I would even say more : If anyone could prove
to me that Christ is outside the truth, and if the truth
really did exclude Christ, I should prefer to stay with
Christ and not with the truth. . . .

This is the most significant passage of all
Dostoevsky's letters, and one not to be superficially understood. Though Dostoevsky lived
and worked for twenty-six years afterwards,
he never surrendered that creed. But what
is that creed ?

It is not a religious creed at all. Dostoevsky
confesses himself the child of unbelief and
scepticism : his doubts never leave him ;
neither does his loving admiration for Christ
the Man. And this loving admiration for the
superlatively human nature of Christ does not
for one moment conflict with his profounder
disbelief. He saw in Christ the perfect man ;
but though he longed, " like dry grass," to
quench his thirst for faith in His Divinity, he
could not. He was in truth the child of unbelief, who with all the strength of his ardent

and passionate nature sought the consolation of faith and found it not. He had looked upon pain, therefore he must deny God ; nay more, his very love for Christ the Man drove him to yet more passionate denial of His Divinity. That being whom he recognised for perfect, than whom " nothing was lovelier, deeper, more sympathetic, more rational, more human," had been made to suffer the last extreme of bodily agony upon the Cross. That suffering which may be the crowning mystery and the supreme evidence of Christ's Divinity for the believer, is for the child of unbelief the stone of ultimate offence.

So Dostoevsky stood, leaving prison, on the threshold of his own inward life, with this double burden on his soul, a philosophy which asked and found no answer, and a religion whose only consolation was to make the agony of doubt more intolerable. Truly he might say at the end of his life that there was only one refuge, one cure for his woe—art, creative activity. Into his art he flung his burdened soul, and though the pain of his thought thereby grew more terrible, he could bear it in the heat and dust of battle with the unknown.

He did not know how much he dared to say, nor how to say what he should dare. It may well be he had not yet dared to speak openly to his own soul. Before the real shock of battle in *Crime and Punishment* came years in which he tried his arms. He was still within the walls of the city of men, still confining himself to the old forms of art and the old morality. The works of this brief period of deceptive calm have a significance of their own, but their significance can be truly understood only when we remember that beneath the calm the thoughts of *Crime and Punishment* were being slowly shaped by the deep waters of his soul.

III

THE UNDERWORLD

TOLSTOI twice makes mention of Dostoevsky
in his letters, strangely late in the day. It was
a poor return for Dostoevsky's generous appre-
ciation of his work that he should have waited
until 1880 to read a book by Dostoevsky ; and
it was stranger still that he should have chosen
out of all the works of his great contemporary,
those two books which are least Dostoevsky's
own. Nor is the manner of his comment less
singular than its occasion. "Lately I was
ill," he wrote to Strakhov four months before
Dostoevsky's death, "and read Dostoevsky's
House of the Dead. I have read much and forgotten much, but I do not know in all contemporary literature, any better book. Not the
manner but the point of view is what is so remarkable ; it is so frank, natural and Christ-
like." And after Dostoevsky's death, he
wrote : "It never entered my head to compare
myself with him. Everything he wrote—I
mean only the good, the true things—was such

that the more he did like that the more I rejoiced. Artistic accomplishment and intellect can only arouse my envy; but a work from the heart only joy. . . . Only a few days before his death, I had read with emotion and delight his *Insulted and Injured*."

This strikes one as a little too ingenuous to be honest. " I admired him and wept over him," Tolstoi seems to say, " because I could afford to. I had no need to envy him. He had no style, no artistic accomplishment, no intellect. I never dreamed of comparing myself with him, because I could not imagine him my rival. Therefore I can freely express an admiration which costs me nothing for the works of this simple, Christian heart." One might think that Tolstoi had chosen the books to pronounce upon like a cunning merchant who carefully takes his samples from a part of the sack where he knows the quality is poor, and adds a generous halfpenny to the ludicrously inadequate price he offers. Thus he gains an easy reputation for the soul of liberality among those who do not know that the bag, like Benjamin's, contains gold beyond price.

Perhaps if Tolstoi had read *The Insulted and Injured* with a little less emotion and a little more care, he would have experienced a little less delight. Even there he might have discovered the seed of that thing which aroused his envy, of artistic accomplishment and intellect ; he might even have felt that the intellect whose traces he had found was a more dangerous intellect than any he had as yet to contend with, and the unpleasant discovery might finally have moved him to procure certain other not wholly disregarded books which Dostoevsky had written in the twenty years which followed *The Insulted and Injured.* He might have read them if only to spy out the enemy, and he might have found that there is a rare kind of intellect which is too great to be cabined even within the spacious walls of artistic accomplishment. Perhaps Tolstoi had read these books and preferred to keep silence about them, for there is a disingenuousness in his kind and condescending letter which cannot be wholly accidental. It is hard to believe that Tolstoi should have lived his life in complete ignorance of Dostoevsky's great works. Or is it that these were by him excluded as not being among the " good things and true " ? But Tolstoi had not in those days reached the embittered foolishness of " What is Art ? " He still envied style, intellect, and artistic accomplishment, and he could hardly have failed to recognise the greatest of these three in *The*

Brothers Karamazov, which had appeared only a year before he wrote his unfortunate letter.

Tolstoi himself was not very intelligent. Had he been, there is a curious conversation between the teller of the story of *The Insulted and Injured* and Prince Valkovsky, which might have given him pause. The Prince at least was no fool. He had risked a fortune of three millions upon the accuracy of a pretty piece of psychological calculation, when he had come to see Natasha and his son Alyosha in her mean little flat, and had given them permission to marry and a father's blessing into the bargain. To an eye less subtle than his own he had risked everything; but he won. The Prince did not risk things; he staked only upon certainties in the amusing game which he saw in life. And the man who can create a Prince who is no fool in such elusive matters as the working of a twofold love upon the heart of an honest and ingenuous young man is himself by the stronger argument no fool. Nor had the Prince merely an unerring eye to the main chance, and a very striking talent for dissimulating his debaucheries. He was a philosopher in his way, whose philosophy the young writer who tells the story, Natasha's first and constant lover (himself no fool), finds it most difficult to refute. The Prince had told him a

beastly tale of a *chef d'œuvre* of dissimulation
after his own heart.

" Foo, how disgusting ! " I answered, listening to
this avowal with repulsion.

" You wouldn't be my young friend, if your answer
were different. I knew you'd say that. Ha-ha-ha !
Wait a bit, *mon ami*, live longer and you'll understand, but now, now you still need gilt on your ginger-
bread. No, you're not a poet if that's what you say.
That woman understood life and knew how to make
the most of it."

" But why descend to such beastliness ? "

" What beastliness ? "

" To which that woman descended and you with
her."

" Ah, you call that beastliness—a sign that you
are still in bonds and leading strings. Of course, I
recognise that independence can be shown in quite
an opposite direction. Let's talk more straightfor-
wardly, my friend . . . you must admit yourself
that that's all nonsense."

" What isn't nonsense ? "

" What isn't nonsense is personality—myself. All
is for me ; the whole world is created for me. Listen,
my friend, I still believe that it's possible to live
happily on earth. And that's the best faith, for without it one can't even live unhappily : there's nothing
left but to poison one's self. They say that that's
what some fool did. He philosophised till he destroyed everything, everything, even the obligation
of all normal and natural human duties, till he had
nothing left. The sum total came to nil, and so he

declared that the best thing in life was prussic acid.
You say that's Hamlet. That's terrible despair, in
fact something so grand that we could never dream
of it. But you're a poet and I'm a simple mortal,
and so I say one must look at the thing from the
simplest, most practical point of view. I, for instance,
have long since freed myself from all shackles, and
even obligations. . . . No, my young friend, if you're
a genuine lover of humanity, with all sensible men
the same taste as mine, even with a little filth, a
sensible man will soon have nothing to do in the
world and there'll be none but the fools left. . . ."

" What isn't nonsense is personality—myself." Prince Valkovsky was evil and cruel
and calculating, but he was himself. His personality was the strong rock upon which he
deliberately builded; he had philosophised
enough to destroy the obligation of all normal
and natural human duties, and there he had
stopped, being a man who still believed it was
possible to live happily on earth. But the
dialectic which had brought him so far, might
go infinitely farther in the mind of another and
a better man—one of the Schilleresques,
perhaps, whom Valkovsky could not endure.

But Dostoevsky did not dare to endow a
Valkovsky with more than the rudiments of
the minds which he was subsequently to create.
In *The Insulted and Injured*, good is good still,

and evil evil, and the double-edged and dangerous words on personality are safely put into
the mouth of a villain of the old school. Valkovsky is the evil presence, that ugly and
bestial thing of which all good people have
heard by report and know nothing ; and
Dostoevsky did not dare to represent himself
as other than they. He held Valkovsky up
to universal execration, and so doing he was
manifestly on the side of law and order and
right living ; nevertheless he could not prevent
himself from making his villain rather too
modern for a villain of the old school. Valkovsky had read something and to some effect ;
he was clever and aristocratic, and the honest
Vanya, while he held parley with the enemy
in the Great Morskaya Restaurant, must confess that he certainly is in his right mind. He
is cynical, exquisite, something of a connois-
seur of language, with a weakness for the social
proprieties ; but still he is a villain, a monster
outside the possibilities of decent humanity.
If he is not punished by the law, that is only
because the law is a clumsier and cruder instrument than the human conscience, and he is
clever enough to avoid the overt acts of which
the law takes cognisance. For all his champion-
ship of social forms and his rank and his consequence, he is an enemy of society and a

corrupter of that goodness in human souls for whose protection society exists.

Dostoevsky takes care not to say a good word for him. At the Morskaya café he speaks the enemy in the gate, and lends him a certain cogency in argument; but he holds him at arm's length that all the world may know that though he has braved the beast he has had no commerce with him. Dostoevsky has passed beyond *Poor Folk*, but apparently only a little. "There is Pain," said the youth; "there is Pain and Evil," says the man. There is the evil suffered and the evil done. "We shall have to work out our future happiness by suffering," Natasha cries to Vanya, "pay for it somehow by fresh miseries. Everything is purified by suffering. . . . Oh, Vanya, how much pain there is in the world!" The pain of the world seems to have been gathered into the gloomy city of Petersburg. The wide country from which these innocent hearts come as they came in *Poor Folk*, does not exist in the same time as that terrible city. The forests, the rivers, the plains, God's wide heaven and the free life under the stars, belong to some age of innocence which has been driven into oblivion by the town. The reality of human life is no longer hidden; the golden haze has lifted, and the broad and generous earth itself dissolved away. The things that are, are revealed in their nakedness. " It was a gloomy story, one of those gloomy and distressing dramas which are so often played out unseen, almost mysterious, under the heavy sky of Petersburg, in the dark secret corners of the vast town, in the midst of the giddy ferment of life, of dull egoism, of clashing interests, of gloomy vice and secret crimes, in that lowest hell of senseless and abnormal life. . . ." Again, there is no tragedy, but only the unending and uncomprehended pain which makes brutes of men and women.

This Dostoevsky had seen and told before ; the sense of it never left him. But as yet there is no evidence of rebellion, or at most it is Nellie the child who rebels and will not forgive. Valkovsky is not a rebel ; he is only an intelligent cynic who has decided that there is no need to respect obligations which he never felt, and makes the most of life according to his beastly desires. Clear-sighted enough to see that one must needs be either a doer or a sufferer of evil, he is also clever enough to be on the winning side. But he is only a fact for all his talent. He is the fact of active evil as Nellie or Natasha is the fact of passive pain. Nellie dies ; Natasha is ruined ; Valkovsky wins his three millions. Less even than before

did Dostoevsky diminish anything from the
reality he saw ; but in *The Insulted and Injured* he sets down only what he saw and felt :
What he thought he hid close within his heart,
while he sought the way of unburdening his
deeper soul, which was his passionate mind.

And within a year or two, after *The House
of the Dead* had been written, he ventured to
reveal something of that which was hidden.
The imaginary writer of *Letters from the Underworld* is a man of thought, and not of action.
He does not live at all, but thinks, and his
thought has paralysed his being, until he can
only sit down and contemplate the world that
is, which he abhors yet can by no means escape.
Evil and pain, they tell him, are the visible
working of the iron laws of Nature : the things
that are must be. " What have *I* to do with
the laws of Nature, or with arithmetic," he
answers, " when all the time those laws and
the formula that twice two make four do not
meet with my acceptance ? Of course I am
not going to beat my head against a wall if I
have not strength enough to do so ; yet I am
not going to accept that wall merely because
I have to run up against it and have no means
to knock it down." This is at last open rebellion, even though it be confined within the
ferment of his own soul. He will not accept

life ; he cannot refuse. To live demands a
grosser soul than his ; for in his acute sensibility the equilibrium which Dostoevsky the
youth had sought between the inward life and
the outward is lost beyond recovery. So
clearly does he recognise the vanity of action,
that the only actions left to him are those in
which he has at least a faint hope of momen-
tarily overwhelming his consciousness with the
extremity of sensation. Therefore his existence
passes in the underworld, from which he makes
sudden and fantastic irruptions into the upper
air of decent normal life, only because he knows
that he will suffer there the torments of the
damned.

These torments are all he has to hope for
from life. If he folds his hands in contemplation, he suffers both from what he contemplates
and yet more from the longing to break the
bands of his inertia and to act, for his longing to
act is infinitely greater than that of the man
of action, not merely because the springs of
action are weakened in him and he desires that
which he has not, but because he is conscious
of his own personality, and knows that he
must assert his will simply for the sake of as-
serting his will. Even the existence of that
will he has to prove to himself ; therefore the
actions of that will are bound to be senseless

and evil and fantastical, precisely because they are crucial. Deliberately to do a senseless or an evil or a fantastical thing is to have asserted one's will in the highest, and to have convinced one's self of its reality, because no power on earth save the individual will could have accomplished it. That is his only reply to the life which he cannot accept. But to do good and to behave sensibly, they say, is in his interests. What does he care about his interests ?

I tell you that there is one occasion and one occasion only when man can wilfully, consciously desiderate for himself that which is foolish and harmful. This is the occasion when he yearns *to have the right* to desiderate for himself what is foolish and harmful and to be bound by no obligation whatever to desiderate anything that is sensible. It is his crowning folly ; it is herein we see his ineradicable wayfulness. Yet such folly may also be the best thing in the world for him, even though it work him harm and contradict our soundest conclusions on the subject of his interests. This is because it is possible for his folly to preserve to him under all circumstances the chiefest and most valuable of all his possessions—his personality, his individuality.

This is a searching dialectic. Doubtless it underlay the evil Prince Valkovsky's " What's not nonsense is personality—myself," but

Dostoevsky had not dared to lend it to him. Nevertheless, the obscure writer of the *Letters from the Underworld* confesses to a similar taste for ugly debauchery. Though his reasoning is ostensibly a protest against materialist and positivist philosophers, it strikes far beyond these obvious enemies. Not only the good of the positivist is impotent before it, but what other good can stand against it ?

But Dostoevsky forbore to draw the last conclusion from his own logic. He left it so that it could be said that these confessions were no more than the ravings of a crazy, morbid mind. There is nothing crazy in the argument, however. Certainly it was only a skirmish before the battle, but it was fought with the skill of a master of strategy, and it was fought on a straight issue : Consciousness *contra mundum*. Of course the writer of those letters was a noxious insect which must be destroyed. But what if, given a certain datum, his noxiousness is inevitable ? And further, what if that datum is nothing less than the possession of that which mankind has come to recognise as the proud differentia of man, of *homo sapiens :* the conscious reason ? Is one who possesses this consciousness in the highest degree and has the courage to act upon it, to be destroyed as a noxious insect by the majority of other men who possess it in a lesser form or not at all ? What if life has reached in the modern man a final form whose destruction by its own elements is inevitable ? What if the good man, the normal man, the sound man, the living man, the social man are forms already superseded by something other which can find only in the underworld a possibility of continued existence, which desires to live, but cannot, because the conscious mind desires to accept life, but cannot ?

The underworldling had thought these things. " True," he says, " the normal man is gross —but then the normal man may have to be gross. How indeed do you know that his grossness is not one of his very best points ? Anyway, I grow daily more confirmed in my suspicion that if one were to take the antithesis of the normal man—that is to say, the man of acute sensibility, the man who hails not from Nature's womb, but from a chemical retort— this comes rather too close to mysticism, a thing which I also suspect—the man born of the retort would sometimes feel so conscious that he was being outclassed by his antithesis, the man of action, that he would come to look upon himself despite his acute sensibility as a mouse rather than a human being. . . ."

Yet wherein is he less than human ? There

is only one answer to this : because he feels
and thinks more than his fellows. It is surely
only a malignant mockery to suppose that a
man who is more richly endowed with the
essentially human faculties than other men,
is less a man than they. Here is the beginning
of an ugly and desperate paradox. It is true
that he knows himself not a man, but a
creature compounded in a chemical retort ;
but he also knows that the chemical process is
that of life itself. He is one of the first of the
new men who by the excess of their humanity
are inhuman ; and upon what power falls the
responsibility of his creation ? " Civilisation,"
he says, " develops nothing in man save an
added capacity to receive impressions," and
he might have added, " and to think upon the
impressions he has received." In himself the
last progress of the human consciousness has
ended in a cul-de-sac.

So he lives in the underworld, his hands
folded in contemplation, brooding upon the
evil which life has wrought in himself. He has
no desire, though he knows that he is a mouse
in their comparison, to have the freedom of
the company of the children of the day. He
envies them, yet he would not accept life on
their conditions, for he is, after all, more a man
than they.

FYODOR DOSTOEVSKY

That is to say, though I envy him, I find the under-world better—yet I am lying. I am lying because, even as I know that two and two make four, so do I know that it is not the underworld which is so much better, but something else, something else,—something for which I am hungry, but which I shall never find. Ah no! To the devil with the underworld! . . .

And this something else is a Way of life. The underworld is only living death. The tormented soul of this mouse-man longs to *be*, to resign nothing of his humanity and yet to live. He longs for that which he knows to be impossible, for something within him whispers that it may yet be possible in defiance of his reason and his consciousness. But since upon these alone he must depend to show him the way to the future beatitude, he knows he will never slake his thirst at the fountain of life.

In the story of *The Falling Sleet*, he tells a ghastly history of one of his irruptions into the life that is, of how he desired and won the love of a simple heart, how he hated the woman who loved him and whom he loved, how he outraged her and drove her away in a final inspiration of devilish cruelty and was left alone once more. It was inevitable : and the secret of its inevitability is in the terrible words which Dostoevsky once used in *The Journal of an Author*, when, protesting against the panacea of love for humanity, he said that "love for suffering humanity in a soul which knows it can bring no alleviation to that suffering, will be changed into a hatred of humanity." That, he said, was profounder, even though they did not understand it, than all the gospels of all the preaching of universal love. And the outcast of the underworld, though he desired to love and to be loved, had within him a stronger desire, that he should not deceive himself or another by love. Love was no remedy for him who suffered from the contemplation of the whole life of which love was only a part ; and truly it was better for the woman that she should have been driven away even as she was than that she should have remained with him or he with her. He was in rebellion against life, and since a man cannot live in rebellion, he did not live. There was no hope for him in life, nor any for one who should unite her life with his. He had deliberately and inevitably put himself outside life ; he chose the underworld, because there was no other place for him, and if, when he yielded to the longing within him to be swallowed up in life, to act and to forget and to live, his action was cruel and revolting, that too was inevitable. His being was set in absolute negation to the life of which love is the noblest part.

But he was a sick soul, a mind diseased, a man corrupted by his own thought! Sickness is a two-edged conception. He was abnormal, it is true, and he and Dostoevsky in him was clearly conscious of the abyss that lay between his nature and that of normal men. But abnormality is not the same as sickness. What is sick cannot be sound, but the abnormal may well be true. What reason is there to suppose that the way of health and the way of truth are the same? We may argue endlessly that we dare not suppose that life should itself contain the principle of its own destruction, but why should it not? What evidence can a man derive from the contemplation of life which could make such a conception absurd? The conception is irrational; but life itself is irrational. Life seems to have evolved the human reason for the singularly irrational purpose of making known its own irrationality. The conception is terrible; life itself is not less terrible.

Mais autres temps, autres mœurs. There is another philosophy descended upon the earth in recent times. It may be thought that Dostoevsky's underworldling would find a stouter opponent in M. Bergson than in the positivists and social reformers of his day. If he had miraculously anticipated the doctrine of the bankruptcy of the reason, he had not known that the way of intuition and instinct was open to him. Perhaps he was not quite so simple. If the reason is bankrupt, man is not the less condemned to use it and to put faith in it. If he would resign its privilege, he cannot for all his desire. He is born to the purple. For better or worse it is his so long as mankind shall continue. And if by reason he has decided that reason is unprofitable, it is not likely to be atrophied by the destructive force of its own logic. Nor can man, still possessed of and possessed by reason, fling himself into the nirvana of instinct and intuition. The underworldling was not so simple-minded though he made the same attempt. Instinct and intuition are not detachable parts of the human soul. They are permeated now by the conscious reason and are changed. The underworldling made the attempt to lose his consciousness in them, with tragedy inevitable for a conclusion. Perhaps there is more real philosophy in his proud and final challenge to the normal, living men, that he, for all his sordidness and unchanging despair, had yet *lived* more than they.

Well, gentlemen, heaven forbid that I should justify myself by seeking to include all my fellow-men with myself ; yet, so far as I am concerned, I have but carried to a finish in my life, what you have never even dared to carry half-way, although you have constantly mistaken your cowardice for prudence, and have constantly cheated yourselves with comforting reflections. The truth is that I have been more *alive* than you. That is all. But look a little closer. We do not even know where present-day reality is to be found, nor what it is called. Whenever we are left to our own devices, and deprived of our bookish rules, we at once grow confused—we do not know what to do, nor what to observe, nor what to love, nor what to hate, nor what to respect, nor what to despise. We grow weary of being human beings at all—of possessing real, individual flesh and blood. We are *ashamed* of being human—we count it beneath our dignity. . . .

He is grown weary of his humanity. He must possess his soul in patience until out of his bankruptcy and impotence a new thing is created : but in the age-long waiting for the miracle what shall he do ?

Dostoevsky, who was the man, had his one cure and his one refuge in creating him after his own image. Doubtless he knew that the solace of this activity might be denied to other men. They might even be stronger men and bolder. Had not even the villain Valkovsky let fall a dangerous word, one dangerous in itself, but altogether too dangerously near the exacter reasoning of the underworld ? " What a man most needs is an *independent* will—no matter what the cost of such independence of volition, nor what it lead to. Yet the devil only knows what man's will——" The rest of that broken sentence is not the next chapter in the *Letters from the Underworld,* but in the rest of Dostoevsky's work. Suppose the anodyne of literary creation denied, suppose a man too strong to remain in the underworld, even though it is not a place but a state of soul, then there might be strange things to chronicle. " The devil only knows. . . ." It is true ; but there have been those—Mihailovsky was one —who were convinced that they had seen the light of the Evil One in Dostoevsky's eyes.

IV

CRIME AND PUNISHMENT

Crime and Punishment is the first of Dostoevsky's great books. It is the first in which he
dared really to state the doubt which tortured
him. Hitherto he had been on the side of the
law. In the sight of men he had done no more
than to lift his head above the wall of the City
of Good and observe the enemy. Perhaps he
had approached it more closely than his fellow-
citizens : he had drunk and eaten with the
Adversary in the Morskaya café, but he had
insisted on paying his own bill. He would
carry that bill away with him if need be to
establish his innocence from all complicity
with the works of darkness.

Hitherto he had been content to state a
simple antagonism, and to pronounce himself
without reserve upon the side of the good. No
doubt for those who read even *The Insulted
and Injured* with clairvoyant eyes, he did protest too much. To them it may have seemed
that he knew rather too much about the

enemy, more than could be learned by a simple soldier in the cause of the simple good. At least he must have been a spy in the enemy's camp, they might have argued, and a spy to have wormed himself so deep into the enemy's confidence, must have subdued himself to that he worked in. The true saint flees the very approach of the evil one, and is affrighted by the faint and far-off murmur of his pinions in the air. He does not wait to look the Old Adversary full in the face, or pause to note the colour of his hair and the expression of his eyes.

But if there were any uneasy at the intimacy of Dostoevsky's knowledge of the dark power, they seem to have held their peace. Apparently the Russian world was well content with the new champion of the old morality. But if they were content, Dostoevsky himself was not. He could not suffer that his expression should so far run short of his knowledge. He must follow out his thought in the language of his imagination—and who knows how much actual experience went to the making of that imagination—wherever it would lead him, for he too was possessed with a devil that drove him to his own fulfilment.

And in the opening chapter of *Crime and Punishment* the gates of the City of Good clang together, and Dostoevsky is outside them.

He is already an outlaw, but a timid outlaw,
haunted still by the memory of the security
which he has left behind him. " ' I want to
do a thing *like that* and am frightened by these
trifles,' thought Rodion Raskolnikov with an
odd smile." A thing *like that*—perhaps it
could never be defined more closely. Certain
it is that there is a vague sense in the mind of
frustrated expectation when the deed is made
actual and Raskolnikov has murdered the
old money-lender, Alyona Ivanovna, and her
simple sister. In spite of all the tremendous
power with which the imagined act is made
real, the disquiet of vague disappointment remains, an uneasy feeling that even a dreadful
murder, perhaps by the very fact of its being so
present and so real, is in the nature of a parody
of the intention, not of the murderer, so much
as of his creator. But the mind cannot work
freely any more ; it is riveted to the concrete
drama which is unrolled before the eyes. The
crime is committed, the murder is done, and
by an heroic accident so done that no suspicion
can fall upon the murderer. He is beyond
reach of punishment, if his will prove strong
and constant in its first resolution.

But though Dostoevsky has escaped from
the city and the gates have closed upon him,
no one has seen him. He will not be the one

to raise the hue and cry. If the citizens persist in seeing in him their most valiant warrior, the very champion of their morality, he will not take it upon him to open their eyes. He is content to be a moral writer, so long as they are content to believe him such. He has gone without the walls to reconnoitre the enemy once more, with the boldness of old experience, and he will bring back a knowledge that is as triple brass to the defenders. He will show that the power of their morality is set on foundations more eternal than the ordinances of man-made law ; he will prove that it stands in the very nature of man himself. Even though Raskolnikov has placed himself beyond the reach of punishment, in a stronghold where the king's writ does not run, yet will he be forced to confess his crime by the torments of his own conscience, and to come forward and accept his punishment and his suffering.

Of course, a capable police-officer, like Porfiry Petrovitch in the novel, well versed in the psychology that cuts both ways, could have told them as much. But the lesson would have been less memorable. It is more comforting to have these assurances from the lips of genius ; and there are no geniuses in Scotland Yard, but only clever men. They might be able to state the law, but they could not prove it in flesh and blood. A Dostoevsky can point the moral in the imperishable stuff of humanity, he can show the very pulses of the heart which drives the murderer to the stool of repentance. By his art they can have the inexpressible consolation of watching the sinner in his self-created agony, of seeing his lips move and hearing the words come " softly and brokenly, but distinctly," from his lips : —

It was I killed the old pawnbroker woman and her sister Lizaveta with an axe and robbed them.

That is enough. The Law is vindicated out of the inevitable workings of the human heart. Even though its officers may fail, conscience flings a wider net than theirs, into which the enemies of society are safely gathered. So can the citizens sleep quietly in their beds.

But Dostoevsky, though he deceived them, did not deceive himself. He knew that in Raskolnikov he had chosen a weak vessel, but one in whom, though the flesh was weak the spirit was willing. Not even Raskolnikov will confess himself repentant of his crime with his own lips. It was *reported* that on his trial " to the question what led him to confess, he answered that it was his heartfelt repentance," and it was added that the audience felt that " all this was almost coarse." Dostoevsky knew that it was not almost, but quite coarse,

quite crude and quite untrue; and having
thrown this sop of the appearance of repentance
to the anxious householders, he had the courage
to express the truth without ambiguity. A
year after his heartfelt repentance, in the solitude of his Siberian prison, Raskolnikov could
confess his heart aloud.

If only fate would have sent him repentance—burn-
ing repentance that would have torn his heart and
robbed him of sleep, that repentance the agony of
which brings visions of hanging or drowning! Oh,
he would have been glad of it. Tears and agonies
would at least have been life. But he did not repent
of his crime.

At least he might have found relief in raging at his
stupidity as he had raged at the grotesque blunders
that had brought him to prison. But now in prison,
in freedom, he thought over and criticised all his
actions again and by no means found them so blunder-
ing and grotesque as they had seemed at the fatal
time.

" In what way," he asked himself, " was my
theory stupider than others that have swarmed and
clashed from the beginning of the world? One has
only to look at the thing quite independently, broadly
and uninfluenced by commonplace ideas and my
idea will by no means seem so . . . strange. Oh,
sceptics and halfpenny philosophers, why do you
halt half-way ? "

" Why does my action strike them as so horrible ? "
he said to himself. " Is it because it was a crime ?

What is meant by crime ? My conscience is at rest. Of course, it was a legal crime ; of course, the letter of the law was broken and blood was shed. Well, punish me for the letter of the law . . . and that's enough. Of course, in that case many of the benefactors of mankind who snatched power for themselves instead of inheriting it ought to have been punished at their first steps. But those men succeeded and so *they were right,* and I didn't, and so I had no right to have taken that step."

It was only in that that he recognised his criminality, only in the fact that he had been unsuccessful and had confessed it. . . .

It is true that even that agony passed, as it could not but pass, away from him who loved life so dearly. He finds an ecstasy of forgetfulness in Sonia's love for him, we are told, and in that ecstasy the burden of his crime and his past suffering slipped silently away from him. His logic is forgotten and his will bent in his happiness : but neither the logic is recanted nor the will denied. There is no hint of repentance, and no more than the doubtful promise of his acceptance of Sonia's beliefs. " Can her convictions not be mine now ? her feelings, her aspirations at least. . . ." That gradual diminuendo, upon which the book closes, is of most dubious omen for the future. Perhaps Raskolnikov did wholly forget his old determination and his reasoning : but to forget is not to repent. Repentance demands an ever-present memory of the sin. The most we can hope for Raskolnikov is that he should be too happy in the present to remember the past, for, if he should remember, the old problem would face him still.

But, long before Raskolnikov had reached the security of calm, Dostoevsky had turned away from him. Raskolnikov was for Dostoevsky, as he was for himself, merely the victim of his unsuccess and of his weakness. He was not even an unsuccessful criminal, but an unsuccessful philanthropist. His will was a will to Good ; he leaned upon a Right. There was no difficulty in winning the sympathies of the world for this youthful Don Quixote, who had ridden forth with the gage of humanity in his helmet, this Saint George who had gone forth to combat with the Dragon for the lives of all men. Did not Raskolnikov choose out with infinite precaution " a louse," a vile insect that preyed upon mankind, and guarded a treasure of gold within its den that might be of bountiful service in the cause of the Good ? In so doing did he do more than that which the very Law he defied may soon by its own ordinance accomplish ? He rid, by murder, society of a pest. Had the victim been other than an old pawnbroker woman who lived by evil usury,

Raskolnikov would never have lifted the axe ;
he would never have dreamed of the crime.
It is in vain that he cries out : —

I wanted to murder without casuistry, to murder
for my own sake, for myself alone ! I didn't want to
lie about it even to myself. It wasn't to help my
mother I did the murder—that's nonsense—I didn't
do the murder to gain wealth and power and become
the benefactor of mankind. Nonsense !

But it is not nonsense. The very stones cry
out, not that this was the only cause, but that
it for him was a necessary consequence of his
act. Only in the magniloquence of his own
conceit, only in the intoxication of his own
vision of himself as a Napoleon, could he dare
to deny it. It is true that the motive was
deeper than this, that he murdered because
" he wanted to have the daring." But that
was his fevered dream. He had already chosen
the lesser part when he began to search for " a
louse " for his victim. He had dreamed of a
will which should trample all things under foot,
for the sake of its own pure assertion ; but he
knew that this was for him only a dream, he
knew that even should he find the courage to
kill the usurer, he would have proved nothing
to himself.

CRIME AND PUNISHMENT

What shows that I am utterly a louse is that I am perhaps viler and more loathsome than the louse I killed, and *I felt beforehand* that I should tell myself so *after* killing her. Could anything be compared to the horror of that! The vulgarity! The abjectness!

The magnificently triumphant will of which he had dreamed, had in the first moment of his conception of his plan, been degraded into a cowardly shivering caricature of itself, a little feeble thing that could not for one second stand alone but must lean upon Right. In the underworld Raskolnikov had dreamed of committing crime for its own sake; in the waking world he was one of the thousands who do evil that good may come. He had never for one moment ventured outside the walls of the City of Good : he was only a Schiller, as Porfiry Petrovitch told him, and a Schiller who was in heart and act the President of the City Committee for Social Reform.

Raskolnikov had done no crime. He had done no more than to transgress the Laws which are human institutions; like a timid child, who holds his nurse's hand, he invokes the Good of All for a sanction to his beneficent destruction. No wonder he does not repent, when he has done no sin. What defeats him is the never slumbering consciousness that he is at the mercy of the law. He surrenders to

111

the dead weight of an enemy, not to any Right. Right is on his side, and that not merely his own right—that is a power he had not the courage to invoke—but a right which any clear-seeing man might recognise, and society itself at no far point in the future ratify.

And because he had done no crime, his punishment is beside the mark. Dostoevsky knew that the fate of a Raskolnikov is a baby-problem. Evil, at this phase, has not yet begun to be. " What is crime ? " Raskolnikov asks himself in the Siberian prison ; and that is indeed the question. If the killing of " a louse " be crime, then crime is only a name, a convention as the laws by which it is defined are a convention. This was not the thing Raskolnikov had dreamed of attempting when he muttered : " I want to attempt a thing *like that.*" Crime, as Raskolnikov knew, was crime for it own sake, the naked working of the evil will. Of this evil Raskolnikov is incapable, and knows himself incapable. His loving friends will tell him that he cannot do evil because his nature is good. It may be so, but Raskolnikov, who sees clearly, suspects that it is because his will is weak.

But what of the man whose will is strong ? Dostoevsky knew that the problem was here, and towards the end of *Crime and Punishment* he turns away from Raskolnikov, whom he has weighed in the balances and found wanting, to Svidrigailov. Svidrigailov is the real hero of the book. Raskolnikov himself acknowledges it, and makes way for him when, in spite of his horror of Svidrigailov, he cannot deny that there is something in common between them. The potentialities of Raskolnikov are made real in Svidrigailov ; the dialectic of the student has been carried to its last conclusion in the person of the man. He enters the book first as the rumour of a sinister presence, of something less and more than man, who has outraged the virgin spirit of Raskolnikov's sister, and done violence to the virgin body of a child. This last is rumour, but he is a power to whom such rumours cling, for they are no more than symbols of the reality which is in him. And it is right that this embodied power should make his actual entrance upon the scene " between a dream and a waking," at the moment when Raskolnikov is passing through the horror, the distorted, malignant horror, of his crime in a vision of sleep.

He drew a deep breath—but his dream seemed strangely to persist : his door was flung open and a man whom he had never seen stood in the doorway watching him intently.

Raskolnikov had hardly opened his eyes, and he instantly closed them again. He lay on his back without stirring.

" Is it still a dream ? " he wondered, and again raised his eyelids hardly perceptibly : the stranger was still standing in the same place still watching him. . . .

Ten minutes passed. It was still light, but beginning to get dusk. There was complete silence in the room. Not a sound came from the stairs. Only a big fly buzzed and fluttered against the window-pane. It was unbearable at last. Raskolnikov suddenly got up and sat on the sofa.

" Come, tell me what you want."

" I knew you were not asleep but only pretending," the stranger answered oddly, laughing calmly. " Arkady Ivanovitch Svidrigailov, allow me to introduce myself. . . ."

" Can this still be a dream ? " begins the next chapter, for Svidrigailov is the incarnation of the evil will. In his creation Dostoevsky had left the city. He was no more a timid outlaw, but a man with the courage of his thought and his full imagination. And Svidrigailov is not only a Dream and a Will, but a Man. He is Raskolnikov grown old, but one who with advancing years has abated nothing of his resolution, that his will should compass all things. He has stood alone with the power which is in him, which is the will to know life

to the uttermost, and by that will to triumph
over life. He has passed beyond good and evil.
He has willed that his will should be omnipotent. Nothing shall be forbidden him. He has
taken his stand against the whole of life to
wrest its secret from it. Svidrigailov is real,
real even beyond reality, and he is also Raskolnikov's dream. To be a Svidrigailov and not
a mere Napoleon—that was the vision which
had haunted the murderer. But Svidrigailov
does no murder before the law, for he knows
that this is no question for him, nor will he
deceive himself by having even the faint semblance of a right upon his side. He is his own
right; another right can only take away from
him and blunt the barb of his question.

And the question is this : Which shall prevail, the I, the self, which I know, or some
power which I know not ? Shall I be forced
to recognise any will beyond my own ? Though
Svidrigailov appears chiefly to be a manifestation of the will to evil in act, he is far more than
this. He appears to us first as evil, because the
deliberate working of evil is portentous to our
minds. Because he does evil things, he is a
monster of depravity. Yet this monster does
good with the same even hand ; he spares
Raskolnikov's sister, Dounia, whom he desires,
when she is at his mercy ; he cares for Sonia

and the orphaned children of the Marmeladovs ; he makes over a fortune to the girl bride
whom he does not marry. In him both good
and evil may be found side by side, yet he is
neither a good man with evil impulses nor an
evil man with reactions to the good. For all
the appearance of contradiction, we feel that
he is not divided against himself but one ; and
the secret of his singleness is his single will.
This he has measured against life and the laws
of life. He has done evil, not because he desired
it, but because he desired to be beyond it. In
the process of his complete assertion, every
fetter upon the working of the will to be free
must be broken, simply because it is a fetter.
The things which he knew to be evil he has
done simply because an instinct within him re-
coiled from the evil : therefore that instinct
must be crushed. He, like Raskolnikov, had
" wanted to have the daring," and he had found
it in himself.

In *The Journal of an Author* and his letters
Dostoevsky returned again and again to the
definition of literary genius as the power which
should bring " a new word " into literature.
Svidrigailov was Dostoevsky's new word. The
creation of this character marks the beginning
of his own peculiar achievement. He was to
develop this conception to heights and depths

undreamed of, to refine it, to make it more and more actual until it should seem that the human and the inhuman were finally confounded.

Therefore we must understand Svidrigailov at all costs. He may be a monster, conjured out of the darkness, but he too is human, too human. Watch him when he has enticed Dounia, whom he loves with a passion of desire, into the solitary room, intending—to do her violence ?—he does not know. But the gleam of the beast began to shine in his eyes, that light in them which months before " had frightened Dounia, and had grown stronger and stronger and more unguarded till it was hateful to her." To defend herself from the horror of this she draws a pistol and shoots at him. The first shot goes wide ; he does not move. The second shot misses fire.

" You haven't loaded it properly. Never mind : you have another charge there. Get it ready, I'll wait."

He stood facing her two paces away, waiting and gazing at her, with feverishly passionate, stubborn, set eyes. Dounia saw that he would rather die than let her go. " And now of course she would kill him, at two paces ! " Suddenly she flung away the revolver.

" She's dropped it ! " said Svidrigailov with surprise, and he drew a deep breath. A weight seemed to have rolled from his heart—perhaps not only the fear of death ; indeed he may scarcely have felt it at that moment. It was the deliverance from another feeling, darker and more bitter, which he could not himself have defined. . . .

He went to Dounia and gently put his arm around her waist. She did not resist, but, trembling like a leaf, looked at him with suppliant eyes. He tried to say something, but his lips moved without being able to utter a sound.

" Let me go," Dounia implored. Svidrigailov shuddered. Her voice was now quite different.

" Then you don't love me ? " he asked softly. Dounia shook her head.

" And . . . and you can't ? Never ? " he whispered in despair.

" Never ! "

There followed a moment of terrible dumb struggle in the heart of Svidrigailov. He looked at her with an indescribable gaze. Suddenly he withdrew his arm, turned quickly to the window and stood facing it. Another moment passed.

" Here's the key."

What was the feeling, darker and more bitter even than fear of death, from which he was delivered ? Dostoevsky knew, and perhaps we too can know. Svidrigailov has dared to face life alone, to measure his individual will against all things. And at the last he is broken. He is conscious of his utter loneliness. He has dared to try the great issue. He has done that he knows to be evil, so that he might know whether there was some power beyond him that should punish. He does know : he has not been blasted. Yes, he would have had a flash of ecstatic happiness thrill his soul, if when he did evil he had been struck dead. But no, nothing. . . .

And that nothing means that there is nothing —nothing for that unconquerable will to will any more. He has put the great question, and the answer is silence, that dead silence in which he can hear every beat of his own weary heart, in which he knows himself eternally alone. And that silence and that loneliness is more than even his heroic spirit can bear. He turns to another being, knowing her loathing, yet hoping too that beyond that loathing there may be a spark if not of love, of some feeling that would show him not finally alone. Twice she fires at him. He does not move. His will remains to him, even though the desire to use it is gone from him. The third time she drops the pistol. Something then remains, one last gleam of hope is fired within him, and he asks in a fever of despairing passion if she loves him, or will ever love him. That hope too is destroyed. He is alone ; he has crossed the bounds of all human experience, in his desire to find whether the burden of Life rests on his will alone, or whether there is something beyond, and he has found nothing. Now one thing remains. Death is untried. He tries it, for it lies in his destiny that he should will all things, and will that he should not be.

But to will his own annihilation is easier than to be assured of victory. A Svidrigailov is not deceived by mortal death. Had he known that self-destruction was the end of all, he would not have waited so long. But what if it should be only another question, and another silence, or something worse than silence.

" But what do you say to this argument (help me with it) : ghosts are as it were shreds and fragments of other worlds, the beginning of them. A man in health has, of course, no reason to see them, because he is above all a man of this earth, and is bound for the sake of completeness and order to live only in this life. But as soon as one is ill, as soon as the normal earthly order of the organism is broken, one begins to realise the possibility of another world ; and the more seriously ill one is, the closer becomes one's contact with that other world, so that as soon as the man dies he steps straight into that other world. I thought of that long ago. If you believe in a future life, you could believe in that, too."

" I don't believe in a future life," said Raskolnikov. Svidrigailov sat lost in thought.

" And what if there are only spiders there, or something of that sort ? " he said suddenly.

" He is a madman," thought Raskolnikov.

" We always imagine eternity as something beyond our conception, something vast, vast ! But why must it be vast ? Instead of all that, what if it's one little room, like a bath-house in the country, and that's all eternity is ? Sometimes I fancy it like that."

" Can it be you can imagine nothing juster and more comforting than that ? " Raskolnikov cried with a feeling of anguish.

" Juster ? And how can we tell ? Perhaps that is just, and do you know it's what I certainly would have made it," answered Svidrigailov with a vague smile. . . .

Not even death has its answer to his question. It is only the one last issue, which, being untried, must be tried. Yet is it the most hopeless of all. The silence in which the great question echoes here, may there give back an echo of laughter, of vulgar, sordid, malignant laughter.

But a will which by willing its own omnipotence has nothing left to will, is a living death. Therefore Svidrigailov goes " his journey," early in the morning, while a thick milky mist hangs over the town, in the presence of an official witness, a little Jew soldier, with a peevish look of dejection on his face and a copper Achilles helmet on his head.

Svidrigailov took out the revolver and cocked it. Achilles raised his eyebrows.

" I say, this isn't the place for that kind of joke ! "

" Why isn't it the place ? "

" Because it isn't."

" Well, brother, I don't mind that. It's a good place. When they ask you, you just say he said he was off to America."

He put the revolver to his right temple.

" You can't do it here, it's not the place," cried Achilles, rousing himself, his eyes growing bigger and bigger.

Svidrigailov pulled the trigger.

" Is there Crime ? Is there Punishment ? " Not in the person of Raskolnikov does Dostoesvky ask these questions, but in that of Svidrigailov. Therefore Raskolnikov's repentance and regeneration is no reply, nor is the foolishly repeated panacea of " Purification by Suffering." Suffering may have been enough for Raskolnikov, though Dostoevsky leaves the proof of that to another story, which he never wrote. It would not have interested him enough to write. In Dostoevsky's eyes Raskolnikov could never have been more than an incomplete Svidrigailov, and once he had found in himself the courage and the genius to grapple with the imagination of Svidrigailov, Raskolnikov was no more than a puppet to him.

In truth those parts of *Crime and Punish-*

ment which closely concern the regeneration of
Raskolnikov, the history of Sonia Marmeladov
and her family, of Luzhin and Razumihin, are
in the last resort unessential. They are hardly
more than the scaffolding which supports the
living idea. The Marmeladovs represent the
existence of suffering in the world ; they are
as it were the embodiment of the fact of pain.
By this awful fact Dostoevsky had been fascinated ever since his eyes had been opened
on the world, and pain is the incessant under-
tone of all his work. By nakedly present-
ing pain continually in his work, Dostoevsky
established the foundations of his created
characters. He himself had looked upon pain.
It had tormented his mind with a problem for
which he was bound all his life long to demand
an answer : " Is there a God ? " Lesser men
who ask this question grow weary of waiting
the answer, lacking the will or the strength to
demand again and again, and fall into a comfortable agnosticism, content enough merely
to be. But Dostoevsky was not so constituted.
Perhaps because his hold on the physical being
of life was weak, or because the fires of his
spirit burnt his body away, he was never for
one moment content merely to be. " I have
been all my life tormented by God," he writes,
and all his life he attempted with all his

strength to answer the question : " Is there a
God ? " Champion after champion he sent
forth on to the bloody field, to contend with
life, as he himself contended, even unto
death.

Of these champions Svidrigailov was the
first. He is as it were the symbol of Dostoevsky's passionate denial of God, when he had
looked on pain. To deny God is to assert one's
own divinity. Therefore Dostoevsky conceived a Man who should have the courage of
his own divinity, who denying a will beyond
his own, should be brave enough to assert his
own will to the uttermost. The frame of Svidrigailov is an unshakable dialectic. If there is
a Will beyond my own it must be an evil Will
because Pain exists, therefore, I must will evil
to be in harmony with it. If there is no Will
beyond my own, then I must completely assert
my own will, until it is fully free of all check
beyond itself. Therefore I must will evil.
This man's bones Dostoevsky fashioned thus
out of his own reason, and from his imagination
clothed him in flesh and blood. He placed him
in life to contend with it, and the end of Svidrigailov was death by his own hand. Svidrigailov found no answer, and he brought none
back to Dostoevsky : perhaps Dostoevsky ex-
pected none, for he knew that his creature was

predestined to die. Svidrigailov was a scapegoat sent from his creator's soul.

Yet that the individual will incarnate should be destroyed in this life was no answer to Dostoevsky's question : for he asked, how shall a man, who has a heart to feel pain and a brain to think and a will to act upon it, live ? Shall he be wholly himself and die like Svidrigailov ? Or shall he, like Raskolnikov, deny the power within him and live ? Raskolnikov was recreant and weak. He had the mind, but the will had failed him. But perhaps that way lay salvation—not, indeed, in the weakness and the failure of the will, but in its complete assertion still. Only let the will be asserted after the pattern of the one perfect man, and be turned not to the final affirmation of the self, but to its utter annihilation. Let a man be created who shall be completely passive, who shall suffer all things in himself, and thereby be not less wholly man than a Svidrigailov.

Of this counter-creation it may be said that Sonia Marmeladov contains the promise. But for all her pathos, Sonia hardly exists. She is certainly not real, as Raskolnikov and Svidrigailov are real, and, in comparison with Dostoevsky's later women, she is no more than a lay-figure. She is not big enough to be the vehicle of the Christian ideal of self-annihilation as a way of life, and Dostoevsky did not attempt to put the burden upon her. When Raskolnikov bowed down to her with the all too famous words on his lips : " I did not bow down to you, I bowed to the suffering of all humanity," Sonia's part was played. She is in herself nothing ; she represents the pain of the world, like a figure in an allegory. Therefore it is of little consequence that she is over-drawn, and her self-abnegation tinged with improbability. And when Raskolnikov says to her : " You too have trangressed . . . have had the strength to trangress. You have laid hands on yourself, you have destroyed a life . . . *your own* (it's all the same)," then surely he speaks in delirium, for what he says is not true. Sonia has done nothing, she has only suffered, and that not by her own will, but by some inscrutable will beyond her.

Sonia is indeed a part of Dostoevsky's story, but in comparison with the idea which he desired to realise, the story in which Sonia has her part is of but little importance. A story of some kind is necessary to the novelist, and Dostoevsky needed one to work upon, since he used the novel form ; but in a deeper sense, Dostoevsky was not a novelist at all. The novelist accepts life and takes for granted the great process of becoming, of evolution and growth. His mind is as it were bathed in the sense of time and succession. Dostoevsky did not accept life; in him there is no sense of evolution and slow growth. His mind is timeless, and his antagonists are not so much men and women as disembodied spirits who have for the moment put on mortality. But their mortal occupations and their earthly history are in reality no more than a device for bringing them into the compass of the artistic form which happened to prevail in his century. As Dostoevsky's art developed and his thought went deeper and ranged farther, we must be prepared to discern in them more and more clearly symbolic figures. They are real, indeed, and they are human, but their reality and humanity no more belongs to the actual world. They have not lived before the book, and they do not live after it. They have no physical being.

Ultimately they are the creations not of a man who desired to be, but of a spirit which sought to know. They are the imaginations of a God-tormented mind, not the easy overflow and spontaneous reduplication of a rich and generous nature. Principalities and powers strive together in this imagined world, and the men and women are all in some sort possessed, and because they are possessed are no longer

men and women. Therefore they are not to
be understood or criticised as real, save in the
sense that the extreme possibility of the actual
is its ultimate reality. Before *Crime and
Punishment* Dostoevsky is a novelist in the
old and familiar sense. With *Crime and
Punishment* he leaves the material world, never
to return to it. The bonds that united him to it
had been at all times slender as gossamer, and
weak as the frail body which kept his spirit
on the earth ; but now he had revealed himself for what he was, a soul possessed with the
agony to know. In Svidrigailov he had conceived a vehicle for his doubts and agonies, a
means of creating metaphysical despairs in
flesh and blood. In the incarnation of Svidrigailov, the supreme assertion of the individual
will in act had been brought to desolation
and emptiness. Another way remained. The
second great struggle against the demon of
despair is *The Idiot*.

V

THE IDIOT

IN *The Idiot* Dostoevsky tells that there was in the gloomy devilish house of Parfyon Rogozhin a certain picture of the Christ, a painting of our Saviour which represented Him at the moment He had been taken down from the Cross. Myshkin said it was a copy of a Holbein and a very good copy : he had seen the picture abroad, and he could not forget it. And Rogozhin, who knew nothing about pictures, who had read no books save that copy of Soloviev's *History of Russia*, which he bought at Nastasya Filipovna's suggestion and cut with a sixty kopeck garden knife —that rough, strong, unread Rogozhin suddenly and inconsequently said to Myshkin : —

" I like looking at that picture." . . .

" At that picture ! " cried Myshkin, struck by a sudden thought. " At that picture ! Why that picture might make some people lose their faith."

" That's what it is doing," Rogozhin assented unexpectedly.

FYODOR DOSTOEVSKY

The gaunt and gloomy house of which that picture is the sinister jewel overshadows the whole of the happenings and all the people in *The Idiot*. The picture itself is the turning point in yet another life than Rogozhin's. In his confession, the young Ippolit Terentyev, condemned to death by consumption, tells how he paid a visit to that terrible house, and describes the picture which Rogozhin had shown him.

It is in every detail the corpse of a man who has endured infinite agony before the crucifixion ; who has been wounded, tortured, beaten by the guards and the people when He carried the cross on His back and fell beneath its weight, and after that has undergone the agony of crucifixion. . . . It is simply nature, and the corpse of a man whoever he might be must really look like that after such suffering. . . . In the picture the face is terribly crushed by blows, swollen, covered with fearful, swollen, blood-stained bruises ; the eyes are open and squinting : the great wide-open whites of the eyes glitter with a sort of deathly glassy light. . . . Looking at such a picture one conceives of nature in the shape of an immense merciless dumb beast, or more correctly, much more correctly, though it seems strange, in the form of a huge machine of the most modern construction, which, dull and insensible, has aimlessly clutched, crushed and swallowed up a great priceless Being, a Being worth all nature and its laws, worth the whole earth, which was created perhaps solely for the advent of that being. This picture expresses and unconsciously suggests to one the conception of such a dark, insolent, unreasoning and eternal power to which everything is in subjection. . . .

And that was Dostoevsky's creed, for it is the necessary end of passionate love for Christ the Man, without belief in His divinity. It is easy to claim Dostoevsky for a Christian, if you do not care to understand his conception of Christ. He loved Christ, indeed, as few men have loved Him; but such a love for Christ will work havoc with Christianity. Dostoevsky never faltered in this love, but the love could never satisfy his hunger for belief. Those two things are sundered by an abyss. It may even be that they cannot in great hearts be reconciled. A Dostoevsky would not purchase the security of faith in Christ's divinity at the price of His mortal agonies. His soul was tortured with the desire for that security, yet would he have refused had it been offered to him, so devouring was his love for Christ.

The vision of Christ haunted him throughout his life. It was a twofold vision. First, Christ was to him the eternal symbol of Pain, and the power of the Beast. He was also the pattern of human perfection, the supreme champion of agonised humanity against the

devil of darkness. In Him, man fronted the
Beast and fought the last fight with him. For
to the mind of Dostoevsky, as to all minds with
so deep capacity to feel and to think, there are
two ways by which mortal man can contend
with the world in which Good and Evil are for
ever intertwined. The one is to act, the other
to suffer. These things are to the outward
eye of opposite complexion : inly they are the
same. In each the individual will is pitted
against the unknown power. The man who
acts absolutely, strives for the last assertion of
his will; the man who absolutely suffers,
asserts his will beyond this ultimate degree,
for he wills that his will should be annihilated.
To suffer nothing, but in all things to act, to
allow no rein from beyond upon the conscious
individual will whether of instinct or of law,
is in intention the same as to suffer all things,
in nothing to act, to bow the will to every alien
power. There is in this no mystery, unless it
be the old mystery of the identity of things
opposite. Each road leads to self-annihilation; for it stands in the destiny of him who
would will all things that he should will his
own destruction. He may, as did Svidrigailov,
will his own mortal death, but that is a hazard,
for he has no assurance that the annihilation
of the physical body will bring with it in an-

nihilation of the will which he is. To will his own mortal death is only a symbol of willing his own death in life, of acting no more, but only suffering.

Such was the champion of humanity whom Dostoevsky saw in Christ the man, who by the way of suffering all things sought to wrest the secret from life. To struggle with life for its secret is for the true consciousness the only way to discover whether a man can live. A way of life for the knowing mind which has looked upon pain—this was the object of Dostoevsky's terrible seeking, and in Christ he saw a way of life. Christ was for him the most valiant, the most noble, the most gentle, the most perfect knight that ever rode forth on the awful Quest; but in him he found no answer to the eternal question. Christ was a man who had asked, not a God who answered, and Dostoevsky loved him. Let those who are so easily content to call Dostoevsky a Christian and pass on, and who read his books as novels among other novels, more curious, more difficult and tiresome than the rest, consider if they can the full significance of the last and most beautiful article of his creed: " If any one can prove to me that Christ is outside the truth, and if the truth really does exclude Christ, I should prefer to stay with Christ and

not with the truth." For in those words Dostoevsky confessed that for him the truth did
exclude Christ.

Therefore, although he truly said that he
would rather stay with Christ than with the
truth, he could not. His seeking spirit drove
him on and would not suffer that he should
stay with Him to whom all his instinct and his
power of love bound him captive. The mind
could not permit the heart's delay. But no
matter to what depths his conscious mind impelled him in the search, the memory of Christ
the man haunted him, with the vision of a way
of life. In *The Idiot* he made the attempt to
embody his vision. The will to act had in
Svidrigailov been shattered in final disillusion ;
in Myshkin, Dostoevsky tried the other way,
the will to suffer.

There is despair, a sardonic and awful despair,
in the very title. To make the conception
of a perfect man tolerable to the sense of
probability in the mind of the world, he must
be represented as an idiot. As a Russian
literary historian most naïvely says : " The
theory put forward in *The Idiot* is, that a brain
in which some of those springs which we consider essential are weakened may yet remain
superior, both morally and intellectually, to
others less affected." Nothing could be wider

of the mark than this criticism, chiefly because it contains so much of the superficial truth ; it is the point of view of one from whose understanding the poignancy of the title is wholly concealed. Dostoevsky himself had a far different conception of his work ; in 1868, when he was beginning to write *The Idiot*, he confessed in a letter to his niece that " the basic idea is the representation of a truly perfect and noble man," not one in whose brain some of those springs which we consider essential are weakened, but one who being perfect and noble must inevitably appear out of the course of nature to the inhabitants of the modern world. Therefore Dostoevsky was bound to represent Myshkin, who was of another kind than his fellow-men, as set apart from them by sickness. He as it were descends upon Russian life from the unknown, which for the sake of material-minded literary historians is said to have been a mental sanatorium in the Swiss mountains. From the standard of the normal, he is abnormal, judged by what passes for health, he is sick ; but does that mean more than that a perfect man must in this life pay the penalty of his perfection ? This is the issue which the creator of Myshkin challenged. If there are in Myshkin's brain certain essential springs weakened, let the charge be proved and the weakness shown. If his life be questioned, and the proof of his weakness be sought in his outward actions, can we hope for keener intuition in his critics than there is in Nastasya Filipovna and Aglaia Epanchin ? While, if the finger be pointed at his manifest disease, do they care to answer this dialectic ?

He remembered among other things that he always had one minute just before the epileptic fit (if it came on while he was awake), when suddenly in the midst of sadness, spiritual darkness and oppression, there seemed at moments a flash of light in his brain, and with extraordinary impetus all his vital forces suddenly began working at their highest tension. The sense of life, the consciousness of self, were multiplied ten times at these moments which passed like a flash of lightning. His mind and heart were flooded with extraordinary light ; all his uneasiness, all his doubts, all his anxieties were relieved at once ; they were all merged in a lofty calm, full of serene, harmonious joy and hope. But these moments, these flashes, were only the prelude of that final second (it was never more than a second) with which the fit began. That second was, of course, unendurable. Thinking of that moment later, when he was all right again, he often said to himself that all these gleams and flashes of the highest sensation of life and self-consciousness, were nothing but disease, the interruption of the normal condition; and if so, it was not at all the highest form of being, but on the contrary must be reckoned the lowest. And yet he came at last to an extremely paradoxical conclusion. "What if it is disease?" he decided at last. "What does it matter that it is an abnormal intensity, if the result, the minute of sensation, remembered and analysed afterwards in health, turns out to be the acme of harmony and of beauty, and gives a feeling, unknown and undivined till then, of completeness, of proportion, of reconciliation, and of ecstatic devotional merging in the highest synthesis of life?" These vague expressions seemed to him very comprehensible, though too weak. That it really was "beauty and worship," that it really was "the highest synthesis of life," he could not doubt, and could not admit the possibility of doubt. It was not as though he saw abnormal and unreal visions of some sort at that moment, as from hashish, or opium, or wine, destroying the reason and distorting the soul. He was quite capable of judging that when the attack was over. These moments were only an extraordinary quickening of self-consciousness—if the condition was to be expressed in one word

—and at the same time of the direct sensation of existence in the most intense degree. Since at that second, that is at the very last conscious moment before the fit, he had time to say to himself clearly and consciously, " Yes, for this moment one might give one's whole life ! " then without doubt that moment was really worth the whole of life. He did not insist upon the dialectical part of his argument however. Stupefaction, spiritual darkness, idiocy stood before him conspicuously as the consequence of these " higher moments " ; seriously, of course, he would not have disputed it. There was undoubtedly a mistake in his conclusion — that is in his estimate of that minute, but the reality of the sensation somewhat perplexed him. What was he to make of that reality ? For the very thing had happened ; he actually had said to himself at that second, that for the infinite happiness he had felt in it, that second really might well be worth the whole of life. " At that moment," as he told Rogozhin one day in Moscow at the time when they used to meet there, " at that moment I seem somehow to understand the extraordinary saying that *there shall be no more time.*"

Thus his epilepsy is a means of conferring upon Myshkin what may be called a metaphysical perfection, as well as of providing an

excuse for his fellow-men to be dubious of his
moral perfection. Indeed the barb of this conception is double and enters deep. Here, Dostoevsky seems to say, is the perfect and truly
noble man in impulse and action. To the
world he must be an idiot. Men will accept
him on no other terms, even in imagination.
Let him then be an idiot not in a merely figurative sense of common language, but in the
medical meaning of the word, in the sense of
" scientific exactness." This twofold idiot has
not merely a way of life which is too high for
the common understanding, but a consciousness
which soars beyond the knowledge of philosophy and in a timeless instant makes mouths
at the questionings of the earthly wise.

But this metaphysical perfection of Myshkin
plays but a subordinate part in the tragedy of
The Idiot. It is as though Dostoevsky had
thereby taken his revenge for the pain which
it cost him to confess that his perfect man must
be an idiot in the eyes of the world, saying to
himself that they who saw in ideal perfection
only the signs of aberration would not know
that in the supreme moment of the consciousness of aberration their whole being, their
little lives, their mean moralities, may have
been engulphed in eternity. They *may* have
been engulphed, for despite the reality of the

one moment which is worth the whole of life,
there is no assurance of the harmony. Life
remains and denies it. And the tragedy of
The Idiot is that human perfection in act even
when it be strengthened with the memory of
the harmony that is beyond life, is impotent
in life itself. The will which wills its own annihilation in a life of suffering comes to no other
end than the will which wills its supreme assertion. The human perfection of Myshkin and
the inhuman perfection of Svidrigailov are
turned alike to derision. To do evil and to
suffer it —each is vanity.

The pivot of *The Idiot* is Myshkin's encounter
with Nastasya Filipovna, who is the incarnation of the evil done in the world. For this evil
Dostoevsky employs one symbol continually,
the outrage done upon the innocence of a child ;
and this symbol returns again and again in
his work to the end. Nastasya Filipovna had
been outraged as a child by Prince Totsky.
For nine years she had brooded upon her wrong,
and those nine years of suffering are printed
upon her face. In the morning of the day on
which he enters life Myshkin sees that face in
a picture, and that first vision of Pain never
leaves him. The story of *The Idiot* is that
Myshkin cannot turn away from that Pain,
neither can he for all his love assuage it, for

his love is pity, and Nastasya is proud. She cannot endure the thought that Myshkin should pity her. Perhaps at the first, when he first saw that face and *those eyes* he did not pity her; perhaps he was instantly in love with a suffering soul. But to love a woman for her suffering, is only to perpetuate her suffering, and to love in her that which is not really her. Therefore Nastasya fears Myshkin; he is an ideal that cannot be translated into reality. A real Myshkin pities, and pity is intolerable. Nastasya had loved and rejected the Myshkin she had dreamed before ever she saw the real one.

" I am something of a dreamer myself as you know. Haven't I dreamed of you myself ? You are right, I dreamed of you long ago when I lived five years all alone in his country home. I used to think and dream, and I was always imagining someone like you, kind, good and honest, and so stupid that he would come forward all of a sudden and say, ' You are not to blame, Nastasya Filipovna, and I adore you.' I used to dream like that till I nearly went out of my mind. . . ."

There is no salvation for a Nastasya. It is right that there should not be. Salvation in this life might make her, too, cry Hosanna ! and glorify the outrage that has been done upon her by evil. She knows that too well in

her deepest heart. Her wrong has isolated
her; every man's hand is against her and her
hand is against every man. She will not stoop
to reconciliation even though it be offered her
in the pure heart of a Myshkin. She prefers
to cherish her wound, and she is right; she
has no right to accept happiness even if it were
possible for her. But it is not. She knows that
too. She is proud and great in her knowledge,
proud of her wounds, proud of her suffering.
Our pity, even Myshkin's pity, is an insult to
her; it takes away from her greatness: she
is for all her life the incarnation of innocence
that has been outraged, of the evil than to do
which it were better that a millstone should be
hanged about a man's neck and he be cast into
the sea. Forgive she dare not, forget she cannot: her great and appointed task is to remember, to open her wounds, to thrust her
hand into them until their pain is intolerable.

But the burden is past bearing. Human flesh
and blood must weary beneath it. To this
woman came temptation, for as much as she
was exceeding weary. To be comforted and to
forget, to cry Hosanna! even though it be in
a voice feeble with smiling tears; with quiver-
ing lips and a mist over those dark and unforgettable eyes to whisper, "I forgive "—so to
put away the pain of memory, and to be whole

again, her wondrous head nestling against Myshkin's breast, his arms about her and his eyes wet and brimming with tears, of happiness and sorrow—happiness that one of these little ones should be comforted, sorrow that a woman should have fainted and laid down her cross.

In such a vision came temptation on the evening of that birthday party. For a moment the woman bowed her head to accept her coward happiness. She stretched out her hand towards the healing draught that Myshkin gave her. Had she taken and drunk, she would have been like to ourselves. We would have been made happy, for we little men are instinct-prompted that there are some things which if a man looks upon he dies. But Nastasya snatches her hand away; she is too great to fall, even though she falters. The weakness passed in a storm as it came.

" Did you really think I meant it ? " laughed Nastasya Filipovna, jumping up from the sofa. " Ruin a child like that ? That's more in Afanasy Ivanovitch's line : he's fond of children ! Come along, Rogozhin ! Get your money ready ! Never mind about wanting to marry me, let me have the money all the same. Perhaps I shan't marry you after all. You thought that if you married me you'd keep your money ? A likely idea ! I'm a shameless whore ! I've been Totsky's concubine ! "

" Do you think I really meant it ? " This woman will not confess her weakness now. She will remain true to her heroic self. She will go with Rogozhin, because that is the way of her high calling, because he has *bought* her, because every one of those hundred thousand roubles falls like a drop of molten metal on the rawness of her wound, because with each separate pang she proclaims that she will endure to the end. She will go with eyes open to her doom, and be the incarnation still of the evil that is wrought on innocence. As she runs down the stairs to Rogozhin's troika, she passes beyond our sympathy, and is transfigured to a spirit with but the outward semblance of a woman.

And she chose Rogozhin, knowing that he would murder her, and that her body would be covered with a sheet, and a wrapping of American leather, and bottles of Zhdanov's fluid be set at her head and feet. For if compassion could avail her nothing, neither could passion. She was not whole any more that she could surrender herself wholly to the dark strength of Rogozhin's desire ; she knew that he, desiring, would desire her wholly, to possess her even to the last limits of her being, and she knew that in her life that could not be. Only in her death could she be wholly his. For

Rogozhin's passion could be satisfied by no less than utter possession, and he knew that while she was alive, and her tormenting memory constantly returned to the vision of her suffering and her innocence, her being would escape his desire. Though she gave herself to him yet she could not be his, for in herself there was a consciousness of the outrage done to her that she could by no means put away. Therefore he knew that he would kill her, and she knew that in choosing him, she chose death. And Myshkin, though he strove to thrust the thought away from him,' knew it too, when he spoke with Rogozhin in the gloomy house, after he had come back to Petersburg.

" . . . Of course she doesn't think so ill of you as you say. If she did, it would be as good as deliberately going to be drowned or murdered to marry you. Is that possible ? Who would deliberately go to be drowned or murdered ? "

Rogozhin listened with a bitter smile to Myshkin's eager words. His conviction, it seemed, was not to be shaken.

" How dreadfully you look at me now, Parfyon ! " broke from Myshkin with a feeling of dread.

" To be drowned or murdered ! " said Rogozhin at last. " Ha ! That's just why she is marrying me, because she expects to be murdered ! Do you mean to say, Prince, you've never yet had a notion of what's at the root of it all ? "

" I don't understand you."

" Well, perhaps you don't really understand. He, he ! They say you are . . . *not quite right.* She loves another man—take that in ! Just as I love her now, she loves another man now. And do you know who that other man is ? It's *you.*" . . .

Because she loved Myshkin, the Myshkin of her dreams, so much, she rejected him. She was afraid of her own weakness and of the longing to forget and forgive which overcame her in his presence. She was afraid of Rogozhin, too, for her resolution to endure her suffering until the end which would be death, could not always be steadfast. Therefore she turns from the one to the other continually, to Rogozhin until the bodily fear of death and the passion of regret for that which she has lost with Myshkin overwhelm her, to Myshkin until she is conquered by the spiritual fear of crying Hosanna and the bitterness of self-accusation for failing of her destiny. Her destiny is the final ecstasy of suffering with Rogozhin ; though she shrinks in terror from it, and the weakness of the woman cannot continually sustain the menace of the spirit, she looks upon it and accepts. To guard herself against her weakness, she intrigues that Myshkin should marry Aglaia Epanchin ; for so she will be safe, and she will have achieved yet one more agony for her wounded soul. It shall be a triumph of agony : on the day that Myshkin marries Aglaia, she promises Rogozhin that she will marry him. " Tell them," she says to Rogozhin, " when they've gone to church, we'll go to church." In this delirium of self-torment, with the awful clarity of delirium, she begins to write the letters to Aglaia Epanchin which precipitate the final tragedy. In these letters Aglaia is innocence personified ; she is not Aglaia, but Nastasya's vision of that which she herself was once, and eternally is. Nastasya is marrying not her rival, but her own girlhood to Myshkin, and the letters are written to her old self. Aglaia is not worthy of them, because she has not paid the price of understanding them. How could she understand this, the deepest of them all ?

Don't think I am abasing myself by writing to you like this, or that I belong to the class of people who enjoy abasing themselves, even if from pride. Now I have my consolation. But it is difficult for me to explain it to you. It would be difficult to explain it clearly to myself though it torments me that I cannot. But I know that I cannot abase myself even from an access of pride ; and of self-abasement from purity of heart I am incapable. And so I do not abase myself at all. . . .

Nastasya is conscious of her mission, but Aglaia, who is young and proud, cannot understand ; and Nastasya when she meets her is filled with a sudden revulsion against the contempt and pride to which she has bared her soul. She flings down the challenge to Aglaia ; let Aglaia say the word and Nastasya will even now bid Myshkin to remember his promise, and he will remain with her. And Myshkin remains, although he knows as Nastasya knows that it will be all in vain.

At the door of the church where they have been married, she leaves him for Rogozhin. Myshkin knows where to seek her, in that gloomy house, where, had she married Rogozhin, she would have had nothing changed. He knocks in vain, and then he waits for Rogozhin to come to him as he must. When they together enter the death-like stillness of the dark house, a timeless moment descends upon their lives in final consummation. The last scene of *The Idiot* is, I think, the most perfect achievement of Dostoevsky's art, in so far as his art can be judged by the standards which he himself shattered and passed on. It is the complete fulfilment and the inevitable end, not merely of a history of human souls, but of an epoch in human consciousness, the epoch in which tragedy is possible. Of tragic art, and the conception of life upon which tragic art profoundly depends, this is the culmination. Tragedy here is taken to a higher power than ever before, and unrolled upon another plane of consciousness. Nothing like to this scene had ever been written before. Judge it by a definition of the tragic hero which has well served the world for two thousand years. Where in Myshkin is "the something of blemish" that should overthrow the nobility of his perfection? Yet, the perfection overthrown, who shall say that his soul is revolted? Judge it by the conception of tragedy which the great nineteenth-century philosopher gave to the world? Is there merely "spiritual waste" in this consummation? Is there not rather spiritual annihilation in the vigil of Myshkin and Rogozhin by the body of the murdered Nastasya?

When Rogozhin was quiet (and he suddenly ceased), Myshkin bent softly over him, sat beside him, and with his heart beating violently and his breath coming in gasps, he began looking at him. Rogozhin did not turn his head towards him and seemed indeed to have forgotten him. Myshkin looked and waited ; time was passing, it began to get light. From time to time Rogozhin began suddenly and incoherently muttering in a loud harsh voice, he began shouting and laughing. Then Myshkin stretched out his trembling hand to him and softly touched his head, his hair, stroking them and stroking his cheeks . . . he could do nothing else ! He began trembling again, and again his legs seemed suddenly to fail him. Quite a new sensation gnawed at his heart with infinite anguish. Meanwhile, it had become quite light ; at last he lay down on the pillow as though utterly helpless and despairing and put his face close to the pale and motionless face of Rogozhin ; tears flowed from his eyes on to Rogozhin's cheeks, but perhaps he did not notice his own tears and was quite unaware of them.

Anyway, when after many hours the doors were opened and people came in, they found the murderer completely unconscious and raving. Myshkin was sitting beside him motionless on the floor and every time the delirious man broke into screaming or babble, he hastened to pass his trembling hand softly over his hair and cheeks as though caressing and soothing him. But by now he could understand no questions he was asked, and did not recognise the people surrounding him ; and if Schneider himself had come from Switzerland to look at his former pupil and patient, remembering the condition in which Myshkin had sometimes been during the first year of his stay in Switzerland, he would have flung up his hands in despair and would have said as he did then " An Idiot ! "

In the last word is contained the abyss which separates this reality from our own. Like Myshkin himself in his moment of highest self-consciousness, we too seem to understand the meaning of the mysterious words : " And there

shall be no more time." Between the timeless
world which descends within the walls of that
dark house and our own is fixed a great gulf
which can be passed only at the price of shat-
tering the human consciousness which is ours.
Myshkin is an idiot : Rogozhin is mad. Rogozhin, we are told, heard his sentence
" grimly, silently and dreamily " ; for the rest
of his mortal life must be no more than a dream.
He has been a pure spirit in the world of spirit ;
there alone he lives and has his being.

This world of spirit that is shown to us in
the last chapter of *The Idiot* is not removed
from ours by any merely figurative difference.
It is absolutely other than our own. In it
indeed are pots of Zhdanov's fluid, sheets of
American leather, and a pack of playing cards ;
for, although the world of spirit is terrible,
it is not magnificent : that were too easy
a satisfaction of the pathetically heroic
dreams of mortality, dreamed when the world
was young. Now it is grown old and wise and
cynical. Remember Svidrigailov's bath-house
with the spiders' webs in the corners, which is
eternity : the eternity in which the pots of
Zhdanov's fluid and the sheets of American
leather have their symbolic part, is no other.

But the condition of entering this eternity
is to have put off or to have transcended

humanity. Myshkin descends into life a spirit.
He is perfect man, but this perfection is a
denial of humanity. Rogozhin is pure passion,
as Myshkin is pure compassion: separated
from his brother spirit, he dreams this life away.
He is not part of this life, a man among men
who dreams of the distant memories that have
haunted mankind since the beginning of the
world; he is a spirit, who dreams this life of
ours, and men and women, the dreamer of the
pitiless and awful dream which is human existence. Rogozhin is Body, as Myshkin is Soul;
they are not men, they have only the semblance
of men, in which the Ideas which they are have
been clothed. And Nastasya is not a woman,
but the embodiment of the idea of Pain. Not
idly does Rogozhin seek Myshkin to slay him,
nor is it mere human fascination that drives
Myshkin incessantly to Rogozhin's side: nor
is it incomprehensible that Myshkin should
confess that only to Rogozhin, his earthly
enemy, has he been able to speak his heart;
nor is it strange that Rogozhin should have
taken off his golden cross and put it about
Myshkin's neck, and Myshkin put his cross of
tin around Rogozhin's, proclaiming that they
were brothers. They are brothers, seeking each
other eternally; the spirits which have been
set in enmity in this dream of life yet know

themselves one ; they alone could speak with each other, of the torments of their dream ; for they are Body and Soul. They are the divided being of the Christian dispensation, the spirit which must mortify the flesh, and the flesh which must kill the spirit. Rogozhin is the way of doing and Myshkin is the way of suffering, the restless spirits that walk up and down the earth seeking their lost unity. They are that which is, the final word of the epoch of human consciousness in which we live, body conscious of soul, and soul conscious of body, each seeking the death of the other, yet each knowing that their last home is in a harmony which is denied them.

And these two spirits, these two Ways, are shattered by the life of which they are the twin foundations ; they are conquered by the spirit of Pain, which is life. Passion and Compassion alike are powerless against the life which is ; yet when they are overwhelmed, they conquer. Passion and Compassion lie down and sleep together like brothers by the side of the Life which they have killed and made their own. That vigil in the dark house is overshadowed by the calm eternity of their conquered oneness. For they, who have been made enemies in the life which is their dream, are brothers again by the body of the life which they have killed. It was Life which divided them, and they by killing life and its Pain, have won their own fraternity for ever.

But that which is victory in the world of spirit is defeat in the world of mortality. Though they are brothers in the place where there shall be no time; in the place where Nastasya has been a woman and is now carved out of marble and horridly still, Myshkin is an idiot and Rogozhin raves; for, though being spirits, they have killed life, being men they are in life and are defeated by it. To kill life in the spirit, is to be slain by life in the body. The human eye which peers beneath the white curtains of the windows of that gloomy room, sees within only death and darkness and desolation. There is no hope of reconciliation between the higher plane of consciousness and the lower; between them time and life itself, which is the measure and the dial-hand of time, have been annihilated. Therefore they are not higher and lower, but only other, and this otherness can in no wise be changed, but only recognised and the head bowed before it. How can that light illumine life, which to shine must be kindled out of mortal death?

It is possible that, as Myshkin had proclaimed when he had looked on life, a moment of this inner light and blinding conscious-

ness of harmony may be worth the whole of
life. Yet it is not life ; it denies life. Where
it exists, life cannot. It may be worth the
whole of life, but the exchange cannot be made.
There is stillness and calm achieved in the end
of *The Idiot*, but it is not the calm which is
vouchsafed to any mortal seeking, for it stands
not merely in death, but in that which is *other*
than life. If it were death alone, the end of
that which we are, then *The Idiot* might be a
tragedy among other tragedies. But the end
of *The Idiot* is not a heightened consciousness,
but another consciousness, of which death itself is no assurance. Therefore there is no pity
in the terror which holds the soul during the
eternal moment of that final scene, no pity even
for him who was the incarnation of pity, but
only the chill of more than mortal despair.
There is no purification of the soul to fuller life,
but only annihilation. Our hearts are not
cleansed, they are frozen ; for these were not
men and women who must inevitably come to
clay, but spirits out of time. Their death
means not the death which each one of us must
expect as his sublunary appointment, but the
death of that in us which dares to confront
death calmly as the price of life, of that which
would regard *The Idiot* as a tragedy and as a
triumph of human art. It is not a tragedy,

because by the unearthly logic of its drama it kills that unconquerable hope upon which the conception of tragedy itself was built.

But Dostoevsky lived on, though he had killed his hope. And living on he fought against his own vision. Once again he fought to deny it. The last time he fought to transcend it.

VI

THE POSSESSED

Dostoevsky's letters tell us more about *The Possessed* than any other of his great books. What they say is little enough, but it is very precious. He had infinite difficulty in writing the book. " None of my works," he writes to Strakhov in 1870, " has given me so much trouble as this one. At the beginning, that is at the end of last year, I thought the novel very ' made ' and artificial, and rather scorned it. But later I was seized by real enthusiasm ; suddenly I fell in love with my work. . . . Then in the summer came another transformation : up started a new, vital character, who insisted on being the real hero of the book ; the original hero (a most interesting figure, but not worthy to be called a hero) fell into the background. The new one so inspired me that I once more began to rewrite the whole. And now when I have already sent the beginning to the office of the Roussky Viestnik, I am suddenly possessed with terror—I fear that I am not equal

157

to the theme I have chosen. . . ." Two months later he tells Maikov that he " has undertaken a task to which his powers are not equal." In yet another three months he writes again to thank Maikov for a criticism of the first part —" They are Turgeniev's heroes in their old age "—and explains his letter to Strakhov. "Stepan Trofimovitch is a figure of superficial importance, the novel will not in any real sense deal with him ; but his story is so closely connected with the principal events of the book that I was obliged to take him as a basis for the whole. This Stepan Trofimovitch will take his benefit in the fourth part ; his destiny is to have a most original climax. I won't answer for anything else ; but for that I can answer without limitations. And yet I must say once more : I tremble like a frightened mouse. . . ."

The new hero who rose up suddenly, like a spirit out of the earth, and drove Stepan Trofimovitch Verhovensky from the stage was Nikolay Stavrogin. He, too, descended like his predecessors from out of a mysterious past into life. The narrative tells us that he was Varvara Petrovna's son and Stepan Trofimovitch's pupil ; but between that childhood and the manhood in which he appears to us, dark and mysterious years have passed in that strange city of Petersburg, which Dostoevsky

158

reveals to us as like that chasm in the earth, the *mundus* where the old Romans communed with the awful spirits of the dead.

And though they cannot tell why, the inhabitants of the provincial capital which is the scene of the drama, are terrified of Stavrogin. They fear him and they hate him, in a frenzy of fear and hatred, as though he were a portent. He did strange things ; he pulled by the nose the harmless Gaganov, who had the innocent habit of saying on occasion that " he couldn't be led by the nose " ; he bit the governor's ear, pretending that he would whisper to him. But it was not for these stupid and outrageous acts that he was hated ; it was for the manner and the intention with which he did them. By some instinct they knew that he was not mad. " The general outburst of hatred with which everyone fell upon the ' ruffian and duelling bully from the capital ' also struck one as curious," says the imaginary eye-witness in whose mouth the narrative is put. " They insisted on seeing an insolent design and deliberate intention to insult our whole society at once." For reasons of which they can give no account to themselves the citizens hate Stavrogin for his *being,* and in spite of their old convictions, it is a relief to them that they can after all ascribe his actions to derangement, when he is seized by a brain-fever while under arrest for the most serious of his outrages.

But they were right before. Stavrogin was not mad. The crafty enthusiast Liputin knew it when he sent his message. And we too now know the nature of the spirit which embodied awakens the unreasoning hatred and fear of society. Stavrogin is one of those who must be taken outside the city walls and stoned until he is dead. Those stupid and outrageous acts were but the trials of his will, for he is Will incarnate. He is utterly alone, having set his individual consciousness against life. He has gone so far on his lonely path that we can see him no more. The far cold distance holds him. In the years that passed between his first descent upon the city and the second, it was rumoured that he had been on an expedition to the icy North. Svidrigailov, too, had talked of such a journey. In the history of both of them this travelling in the cold and silent wastes of the earth was only a symbol, by which Dostoevsky could convey in temporal terms, the lonely and infinite distance to which their spirit had been driven. The chill, still desolation of the timeless world to which Stavrogin has ruthlessly pursued his way, hangs about him, striking terror into the heart of his own mother.

He remained standing for two minutes in the same position by the table, apparently plunged in thought, but soon a cold and listless smile came on to his lips. He slowly sat down again in the same place on the corner of the sofa, and shut his eyes as though from weariness. . . . Varvara Petrovna knocked at the door gently as before, and again receiving no answer, she opened the door. Seeing that Nikolay Vsyevolodovitch was sitting strangely motionless, she cautiously advanced to the sofa with a throbbing heart. She seemed struck by the fact that he could fall asleep so quickly and that he could sleep sitting like that, so erect and motionless, so that his breathing even was scarcely perceptible. His face was pale and forbidding, but it looked as it were numb and rigid. His brows were somewhat contracted and frowning. He positively had the look of a lifeless wax figure. She stood over him for about three minutes, almost holding her breath, and suddenly she was seized with terror. . . .

The cold horror of that portrait is terrible. Stavrogin is not a man, but a presence. He has looked upon the frozen waste of eternity. We cannot see him ; his physical body is only a shell. His spirit is infinitely away. We can follow the road he has gone only by the vision of his dead selves, Kirillov and Shatov and Pyotr Verhovensky. These are the things he has passed beyond, and having passed beyond them, he is lost to sight. To each of these men he has been a leader and a God : each of them, in his supreme moment, cries to Stavrogin in the same words : " Remember how much you have meant in my life ! " Even the pitiful Lebyadkin, who had crossed his path in the dark Petersburg days, echoes the words ; though of what Stavrogin had taught him, he can express only a remembered, yet significant phrase. " One must really be a great man even to make a stand against common sense." That rang in Lebyadkin's memory ; it was the oracle delivered to him by his God. And Lebyadkin had known by sure instinct that Stavrogin had had this greatness. Was it not upon his own sister, the cripple and demented Marya Timofeyevna, that Stavrogin had made trial of it ?

" It takes a great man to make a stand even against common sense." It was worth remembering, for even though the message was apportioned to Lebyadkin's understanding, it yet contained all Stavrogin's secret. To have the instinct of common sense in his heart, and to trample upon it just because it was an instinct, and therefore an impediment to the working of his conscious will ; to sacrifice all things to his will, all instincts, all impulses, all emotions, all loves, all loyalties ; to know himself apart from life and to stamp out the embers of the flame in his soul ; to be in all things conscious, since to yield to that which was unconscious was to declare himself a slave to the life which he hated and denied; to will that his own will should be the master absolute of all things—" it takes a great man to make a stand even against common sense." And there were impulses more overwhelming even than common sense.

There is the anger of pride. Nikolay Stavrogin was proud. " You are beautiful and proud as a God," says Pyotr Verhovensky to him. His pride was superhuman, as his will. Yet when his will demanded that his pride should yield, he broke his pride. So when Shatov struck him, he withheld his hand.

He had scarcely regained his balance after being almost knocked over in this humiliating way, and the horrible as it were sodden thud of the blow in the face had scarcely died away in the room when he seized Shatov by the shoulders with both hands, but at once, almost at the same instant, pulled both hands away and clasped them behind his back. He did not speak, but looked at Shatov, and turned as white as his shirt. But strange to say the light in his eyes seemed to die out. Ten seconds later his eyes looked cold, and I'm sure I'm not lying—calm. Only he was terribly pale. Of course I don't know what was passing within the man, I saw only his exterior. It seems to me that if a man should snatch up a bar of red-hot iron and hold it tight in his hand to test his fortitude, and after struggling for ten seconds with insufferable pain end by overcoming it, such a man I fancy would go through something like what Nikolay Vsyevolodovitch was enduring those ten seconds. . . .

"But, strange to say, the light in his eyes died out." But was it strange? The will of Lucifer had broken Lucifer's pride. Stavrogin had put upon himself the last torment of all and had endured it. Pride was the unconscious form of his triumphant conscious will, and that too he had crushed. Yet not even for that would the light of his eyes have grown dim. He had struck at the inmost of his being, because he willed the omnipotence of his will; and in the very moment of his triumph he knew that it was of no avail. In his soul each succeeding victory could bring only instant desolation, and this was the last desolation of all. When he had killed his pride, he had killed even that which had urged him to kill his pride. The spring of the will itself was broken. There was not only nothing left to will, but of the will itself nothing remained.

That moment was the pinnacle of his assertion of his will. Beneath it were ranged all the other trials which he had imposed upon his unconquerable will. His rumoured debauchery in Petersburg, which was not debauchery but the assertion of his conscious will against the instinct for good whose sovereignty he could not accept ; his marriage with the demented cripple, which was the triumph of his will, not over common sense, but over the innate sense of harmonious beauty which resides in all great souls ;—these were trials which only his pride could give him strength to sustain. By that he had found in himself the power to pass within his own soul beyond good and evil, beyond beauty and ugliness. There remained one instinct to him, upon which his whole desperate life was built, the instinct of pride. This instinct he had himself created. It was the unconscious counterpart of his conscious will to assertion. It had grown strong with his triumphs. It had borne him beyond good and evil, beyond beauty and ugliness. It bore him now beyond itself, beyond pride and submission ; and his spirit died within him. "Only he was terribly pale." The last, the only virtue had gone out of him.

After this moment, Stavrogin in the land of living is dead. He has submitted himself to the last mortification of the flesh. He is now conscious will and nothing more ; he is not even incarnate, seeing that the extreme assertion of consciousness itself depends upon supporting instinct. He had killed his last instinct, and by the act he is become a pure spirit. He is will that cannot work its will any more. There is no more contact between him and the physical world which is the vehicle of life.

So Nikolay Stavrogin dies on the day that he makes his first appearance in the body in the story of *The Possessed*. For a moment, as it were, in the supreme incandescence of his earthly struggle, he puts on surpassing human beauty. " Now—now, I don't know why," says the narrator, " he impressed me at once as absolutely, incontestably beautiful, so that no one could have said that his face was like a mask. Wasn't it perhaps that he was a little paler, and seemed rather thinner than before ? . . ." But Dostoevsky could not tolerate the grossness of his imaginary narrator's vision, and despite himself, he adds : " Or was there perhaps the light of some new idea in his eyes ? " And we know what was this new idea. His eyes shone with the joyous expectation of the final battle ; he was elate with his own determination to make his pride bow to his will. He had come determined to publish abroad his marriage with the half-witted cripple. To have married her in secret was his victory over his own sense of ugliness ; to proclaim his marriage would be the triumph over his pride. But when he entered the room, the occasion had been taken out of his hands. Whether his

pride was too great to be thus suddenly overthrown, or whether his mother's instant question diminished from his own will, he was
silent. And Shatov, for whom he was a God,
felt the *lie* in his silence, and struck him before
them all, before Lise, and Darya, his lovers,
and before his mother. Shatov struck his God
for failing of his Godhead, and this time his
God did not fail. Stavrogin held his hand;
the final victory was won, and the light of the
new idea died down in his eyes. The moment
of his absolute beauty passed, and his face became a mask again.

The story of *The Possessed* passes between
this death of the spirit of Stavrogin and the
death of his body. He has no fear of bodily
death; then he might kill himself, to conquer
the fear. He has no hope in death; he is only
afraid that he might deceive himself with such
a hope. " I know I ought to kill myself," he
writes to Darya Shatov before the end, " to
brush myself off the earth like a nasty insect;
but I am afraid of suicide, for I am afraid of
showing greatness of soul. I know it will be
another sham again—the last deception in an
endless series of deceptions. What good is
there in deceiving one's self? Simply to play
at greatness of soul? " And in the brief time
of his phantom life, his life in death, which

remained to him, he is haunted by the souls that he himself has created, by Kirillov and Shatov and Pyotr Verhovensky. He, the God, has fashioned these men, and given them life, while he himself is dead. They believe in the creeds which he has given them, and believing, they live. But they believe the creeds because they believe in the man.

At the end of the strange and terrible scene between Stavrogin and Shatov, which must have cost Dostoevsky an agony to write, Shatov cries out : —

" Stavrogin, why am I condemned to believe in you through all eternity ? Could I speak like this to any-one else ? I have modesty, but I am not ashamed of my nakedness because it's Stavrogin I'm speaking to. I was not afraid of caricaturing a grand idea by hand-ling it because Stavrogin was listening to me. . . . Shan't I kiss your foot-prints when you've gone ? I can't tear you out of my heart, Nikolay Stavrogin."

The grand idea which Stavrogin had given to him and he had learned by heart in Stavrogin's words was this : —

" Not a single nation has ever been founded on principles of science or reason. There never has been an example of it, except for a brief moment, through folly. Socialism is from its very nature bound to be atheism, seeing that it has from the very first pro-claimed that it is an atheistic organisation of society, and that it intends to establish itself exclusively on the elements of science and reason. Science and reason have from the beginning of time played a secondary and subordinate part in the life of nations ; so will it be till the end of time. Nations are built up and moved by another force which sways and dominates them, the origin of which is unknown and inexplicable : that force is the force of an insatiable desire to go on to the end, though at the same time it denies that end. It is the force of the persistent assertion of one's own existence and a denial of death. It's the spirit of life, as the Scriptures call it, the ' river of living water,' the drying up of which is threatened in the Apocalypse. It's the æsthetic principle as the philosophers call it, the ethical principle with which they identify it, ' the seeking for God ' as I call it more simply. The object of every national movement in every people and at every period of its existence is only the seeking for its god, who must be its own god, and the faith in Him as the only true one. God is the synthetic personality of the whole people, taken from its beginning to its end. It has never happened that all or even many people have had one common god, but each has always had its own. It's a sign of the decay of nations when they begin to have gods in common. When gods begin to be common to several nations the gods are dying and the faith in them together with the nations themselves. The stronger a people the more individual their god. There never has been a nation without a religion, that is without an idea of good and evil. Every people has its own conception of good and evil, and its own good and evil. When the same conceptions of good and evil become prevalent in several nations, then these nations are dying, and then the very distinction between good and evil is beginning to disappear. Reason has never had power to define good and evil, or even to distinguish between them even approximately; on the contrary, it has always mixed them up in a disgraceful and pitiful way; science has even given the solution by the fist. This is particularly characteristic of the half-truths of science, the most terrible scourge of humanity, unknown till this century and worse than plague, famine or war. A half-truth is a despot such as has never been in the world before. A despot that has its priests and slaves, a despot to whom all do homage with love and superstition hitherto inconceivable, before which science itself cringes and trembles in a shameful way. These are your own words, Stavrogin, all except that about the half-truth; that's my own because I am myself a case of half-knowledge, and that's why I hate it particularly. I haven't altered anything of your ideas or even of your words, not a syllable."

" I don't agree that you've not altered anything," Stavrogin observed cautiously. " You accepted them with ardour, and in your ardour have transformed them unconsciously. The very fact that you reduce God to an attribute of nationality . . ."

He suddenly began watching Shatov with intense and peculiar attention, not so much his words as himself.

" I reduce God to an attribute of nationality ? " cried Shatov. " On the contrary, I raise the people to God. And has it ever been otherwise ? Every people is only a people so long as it has its own god and excludes all other gods on earth irreconcilably; so long as it believes that by its god it will conquer and drive out of the world all other gods. Such, from

the beginning of time, has been the belief of all great
nations, all anyway who have been specially remarkable, all who have been leaders of humanity. . . . A
really great people can never accept a secondary part
in the history of Humanity, nor even one of the first,
but will have the first part. A nation which loses this
belief ceases to be a nation. But there is only one
truth and therefore only a single one out of the nations
can have the true God, only one nation is ' god-bear-
ing,' that's the Russian people, and . . . and . . .
and can you think one such a fool, Stavrogin," he
yelled frantically all at once, " that I can't distinguish
whether my words at this moment are the rotten old
commonplaces that have been ground out in all the
Slavophil mills in Moscow, or a perfectly new saying,
the last word, the sole word of renewal and resurrection, and . . . what do I care for your laughter at
this minute ! What do I care that you utterly fail to
understand me, not a word, not a sound. . . ."

These words had need to be quoted in their
fullness ; for they are Dostoevsky's public
profession of faith. They contain the substance
of all that Dostoevsky, when he wrote as
a publicist, professed to believe. In *The
Possessed*, he dared, rather by the force of his
own inward sincerity he was compelled, to
represent them as the discarded beliefs of
Nikolay Stavrogin. With these words Stavrogin had sowed the seed of God and the father-
land in Shatov's heart, while he lay on straw
beside Kirillov in America. With them he had

raised Shatov from the dead. Yet, " perhaps
at that very time, perhaps during those very
days," Shatov says to him, " I have learnt that
you were infecting the heart of that hapless
creature, that maniac Kirillov, with poison . . .
you confirmed malignant ideas in him, and
brought him to the verge of madness." There
may at some other time be occasion to consider the political and religious faith to which
Dostoevsky gave public expression. But the
essence of the matter lies here. The public
Dostoevsky was Shatov, the real Dostoevsky
Stavrogin, or rather since his mind conceived
Stavrogin, a spirit that passed even beyond
this. And it is well to remember that in this
chapter we may hear the real Dostoevsky
putting the final question to the public one :
" Have you caught your hare ? "

" I only wanted to know, do you believe in God,
yourself ? "

And what does the public one reply ?

" I believe in Russia. . . . I believe in her orthodoxy. . . .I believe in the body of Christ . . . . I believe
that the new Advent will take place in Russia. . . . I
believe. . . ." Shatov muttered frantically.
" And in God ? in God ? "
" I . . . I *will* believe in God ! "

Shatov is not big or strong enough to face
his own unbelief. Though he knows that he

cannot believe in God, he can almost deceive himself with a Gospel of Russia. But his belief in that Gospel depends not upon his belief in God but upon his belief in his Stavrogin, who even while he was like a Teacher instructing his disciple in the gospel of salvation through Russia, was pouring a bitter poison into the ears of Kirillov, a gospel in which the strange childlike and brave man, of incomprehensible speech, had also found illumination and ecstasy.

This creed of Kirillov's is the dialectic of a Stavrogin received into a simple mind. If there is no God, as there can be no God, seeing that this life is pain and terror, then I am God. If there is no will greater than mine and including it, then my will is omnipotent. Therefore a man must be found to express his own omnipotent will on " the most vital point," a man who will kill himself just to assert his own will. So will he himself become God, for now God is the pain of the fear of death.

" He who will conquer pain and terror will himself become a god. Then there will be a new life, a new man ; everything will be new . . . then they will divide history into two parts : from the gorilla to the annihilation of God and from the annihilation of God to . . ."

" The Gorilla ? "

FYODOR DOSTOEVSKY

" To the transformation of the earth and man physically. Man will be God, and will be transformed physically, and the world will be transformed and things will be transformed and all thoughts and feelings. . . ."

Kirillov will be the man who shall take upon himself the burden of this symbolic death on behalf of all men. He will be the first of the men-Gods, and in him will perish that epoch of the human consciousness in which man was afraid of the pain of the fear of death, and sought belief in God and in the assurance of immortality to sustain him. The new man will live in the timeless world ; he will have within him the living knowledge of the eternal harmony. For Kirillov, by long brooding upon his determination, has been in the ecstasy of contemplation rapt to the timeless world.

Kirillov came out of his reverie and, strange to say, spoke far more coherently than he usually did ; it was clear that he had formulated it long ago and perhaps written it down.

" There are seconds—they come five or six at a time —when you suddenly feel the presence of the eternal harmony perfectly attained. It's something not earthly—I don't mean in the sense that it's heavenly —but in that sense, that man cannot endure it in his earthly aspect. He must be physically changed or die. This feeling is clear and unmistakable ; it's as though you apprehend all nature and suddenly say,

' Yes, that's right.' God, when he created the world, said at the end of each day of creation, ' Yes, it's right, it's good.' It . . . it's not simply being deeply moved, but simply joy. You don't forgive anything because there's no more need of forgiveness. It's not that you love—oh, there's something in it higher than love—what's most awful is that it's terribly clear and such joy. If it lasted more than five seconds the soul could not endure it and must perish. In those five seconds I live through a lifetime, and I'd give my whole life for them, because they are worth it. To endure ten seconds one must be physically changed. I think man ought to give up having children—what's the use of children when the goal's been obtained ? In the gospel it is written that there will be no child-bearing in the resurrection, but that men will be like the angels of the Lord. That's a hint. . . ."

Kirillov is happy ; but the reasoning to which he will sacrifice his life will not hold. Stavrogin, who planted the seeds of his wisdom in his heart, could not have deceived himself with it. Stavrogin could not lose his reason ; he knew that mortal death was no assurance of the eternal harmony, and he knew also that to kill himself with his own hands was not the vital point wherein man's self-will must be asserted. To kill himself were easy, even a joyful consummation, if it might be done in the belief that a new consciousness would descend upon the world. But that is not self-will ; that

is only to sacrifice one's self, as Raskolnikov
had done, for the good of humanity. By such
a death the individual will is sacrificed, not
asserted. Kirillov had only denied one god, to
believe in another which Stavrogin had created
for him—the dawn of a new consciousness
wherein man should eternally behold the eternal
harmony and be transfigured in the flesh.

This new god of Stavrogin's creation was
and is a possibility. Stavrogin had contemplated the possibility. To Kirillov he had
shown one side, to Shatov another. Shatov's
belief in the Second Advent, and Kirillov's belief in the physical transfiguration of man that
he may be able to behold the eternal harmony,
are the same. Stavrogin, who had pondered
all things, had pondered the Apocalypse.

" You've begun to believe in a future eternal
life ? " he asks Kirillov.

" No, not in a future eternal life, but in eternal life
here. There are moments, you reach moments, and
time suddenly stands still, and it will become eternal.'
" You hope to reach such a moment ? "
" Yes."
" That'll scarcely be possible in our time," Nikolay
Vsyevolodovitch responded slowly and as it were
dreamily : the two spoke without the slightest irony.
" In the Apocalypse the angel swears that there will'
be no more time."

There was indeed no irony in Stavrogin's words then. The possibility of the miracle of a new consciousness was all that was left to him. But that miracle " will scarcely be possible in our time " ; no act of his could give him assurance of it. Kirillov might be able to believe in it and make it his God. Stavrogin could not ; he could not bow down to a god of his own creation.

But, though he could not believe in that which he contemplated, there was no irony in him when he spoke to Kirillov of the new epoch when there should be no more time. Neither had there been irony in him when he taught them both while they lay on straw in America. This Shatov could not understand ; he could not see that the poison with which Stavrogin had infected Kirillov's heart was the very elixir of life when poured into his own. Much less could he understand what seemed to him the enigmatic words of Stavrogin : " I wasn't joking with you then ; in persuading you I was perhaps more concerned with myself than with you. . . . I repeat I was not deceiving either of you." Yet those words contained the simple truth. He was desperately concerned with himself. He, who was in himself the man-God, who knew that the way of assertion of his individual will was not the broad path of

self-destruction, but the hard and narrow one
of passing within his own soul beyond good
and evil, beyond beauty and ugliness, and
finally beyond pride and submission, and had
the greatness and the courage in himself to
tread the way to his divinity—this man-God's
belief in his own godhead failed him. He had
lost, for the moment, his one belief, in the omnipotence of his will. If having lost belief he
could make another human being who had lost
belief, believe, then he might in their conviction
find the conviction of his own divinity again.
Shatov and Kirillov were his desperate experiments. For their belief he offered them
all that he had, the surmise of the possibility
of a new consciousness ; outside himself there
was nothing beside this. He himself was, he
knew, the very culmination of consciousness
as it is now, the last embodiment of the
spirit of the present Dispensation. Therefore
there were two things, and two alone, in
which he might believe—the omnipotence of
his own will, and a consciousness which should
transcend the present consciousness of man ;
his own divinity and the second Advent ;
himself as the final possibility of the present
Dispensation and the New Dispensation. No
matter in which Shatov and Kirillov should
believe, they would believe in him. They

would believe in him first because he had created their Gods, and secondly because their belief in a new consciousness inevitably implied belief in him as the last perfection of the old.

Of such experiments Stavrogin's life had consisted. This was the most subtle of them all ; but there were others. *The Possessed* is as it were littered with the bodies of the living souls which Stavrogin had used for his own purposes. The third man, besides Kirillov and Shatov, is Pyotr Verhovensky. This cunning, terrible man who puts the cruel machinery of his " quintet " in motion, is Stavrogin's slave. " Stavrogin, you are beautiful," he cries ecstatically. " Do you know you are beautiful. . . . You are my idol. . . ." Looking at the face of his proud and beautiful God, he has conceived a plan for the destruction of the world and the creation upon its ruins of a new and harmonious kingdom with Stavrogin for its ruler and its divinity. In Stavrogin he has seen that " absolute beauty " which is not of this world, and he believes that he has but to reveal Stavrogin to the Russian world as the Ivan the Tsarevitch, who lives in legend, for the people to fall down and worship him. Brooding upon this ecstatic vision of a new heaven and a new earth with Stavrogin for its saviour, Pyotr has become crazy with fanatical enthusi-

asm, and he is not only demented but inspired.
The torrent of despairing, pleading, threaten-
ing words which he pours out before Stavrogin
when he reveals his plan, leaps at moments to
flashes of a sublime beauty. . . . " Russia will
be overwhelmed with darkness and the earth
will weep for its old gods. . . ." In the service
of this vision of destruction and recreation, he
is cunning and brave and merciless : his secret
machinations undermine the whole city. But
he does not understand that he and his society
are for Stavrogin only a means of experiment,
one more trial of others' belief in him ; Pyotr
only feels Stavrogin's power, his superhumanity
and unearthly beauty, and he works like a
blind mole to hold him fettered to the
great, fantastic scheme of which he is to be the
prophet. He does not understand Stavrogin
because he is the slave of a Stavrogin whom he
has imagined for himself. " Here now," says
Fedka the convict of Pyotr, " he knows about
me that I'm awfully keen to get a passport
—so he thinks that he's snared my soul. I
tell you, sir, life's a very easy business for
Pyotr Stepanovitch, for he fancies a man to
be this and that and goes on as if he was."
So, too, he thinks that he can snare Stavrogin's
soul, because he knows that he has some mysterious need of Lise. He works to implicate

him somehow in the murder of his cripple wife,
as he grappled the quintet to him by making
them partake with him in the killing of Shatov.
But he does not know that Stavrogin is a spirit
whom no power on earth can hold, who, though
he envies Pyotr for the delusion of his hopes,
holds all his plots and intrigues in the extreme
of contempt. Even Pyotr, like his fellow-
slaves, Shatov and Kirillov, has not seen the
real face of his god. By an uncomprehended
instinct he knows that Stavrogin is the final
form of the dispensation under which we live ;
therefore his brain tells him that he must be
the prophet of the new order. But in moments
of inspiration, he speaks some words to Stavrogin, which show that he had had a vision of
their true relation. " I am a buffoon," he says
to him, when Stavrogin has confessed to Lise
his knowledge of the murder of his wife, " but
I don't want you, my better half, to be one.
Do you understand ? " For Pyotr really is
an earthly caricature of that which Stavrogin's
spirit is. All Stavrogin's dreams that belong
like himself to the timeless world have in Pyotr
put on a crude material garment. Pyotr
dreams of earthly destruction and recreation ;
Stavrogin knows that these things are possible
only in the world of spirit. Pyotr devotes himself to his vision of a future strongly built of

stone ; out of earthly chaos earthly harmony
will rise. That is no more than the coarse and
visible sign of that for which Stavrogin in his
own soul had striven. But Pyotr did not know
this ; in a second of vision he saw himself as
Nikolay Stavrogin's "monkey," but he saw
no more.

Not one of Stavrogin's creatures understands
him. He is beyond them, they know, and they
are condemned to believe in him eternally.
They grope blindly after the secret of their
divinity. Shatov, too, has his moment of insight.

"I don't know either why evil is hateful and good
beautiful ; but I know why the sense of that distinction is lost in people like the Stavrogins," Shatov
persisted, trembling all over. "Do you know why
you made that base and shameful marriage ? Simply
because the shame and senselessness of it reached the
pitch of genius ! Oh, you are not one of those who
linger on the brink. You fly head foremost. You
married from a passion for martyrdom, from a craving
for remorse, through moral sensuality. It was a
laceration of the nerves. Defiance of common sense
was too tempting. Stavrogin and a wretched half-
witted crippled beggar ! When you bit the governor's
ear, did you feel sensual pleasure, you idle, loafing
little snob ? Did you ? "

Shatov was indeed "something of a psycho-
logist," but he was mistaken ; he could not

comprehend the lonely majesty of his deity, though he felt it within him. Instinctively he knew there was some terrible purpose in Stavrogin's denial of good and evil and beauty and ugliness; but what that purpose was was hidden from him. And of what Stavrogin had done in holding his hand and not killing him outright he had no inkling. Nor did Kirillov know more. He felt that Stavrogin was " seeking a burden " ; but he did not know what manner of burden it was, nor did he know, when he rode so clumsily away from the duel with Gaganov, slipping all the while from his saddle, that there were no more burdens for Stavrogin to bear. Therefore, when he bade good-bye to Stavrogin, and shook hands with him to show he was not angry, he could not tell that Stavrogin was appealing to him, not for moral approbation, but for understanding, aye and love. Stavrogin was weak with the loneliness of his exceeding strength, when he said to Kirillov : " I know I'm a worthless character, and I don't pretend to be a strong one." But there was a bitter tragedy in the unconscious irony of Kirillov's reply : " You'd better not ; you're not a strong person." Kirillov had never dreamed even of the possibility of such strength as Stavrogin's ; he had courage because he had no reason. He went

to his death in the strong happiness of devotion
to an idea whose falsity he could not see.
Stavrogin was weak because he was so strong
that he could not deceive himself. Yet because
Kirillov was simple, Stavrogin leaned upon
him for a moment, when he fainted on his
lonely way : for even simplicity is strength.
But Kirillov's simplicity could avail him
nothing. Kirillov was not only too simple to
understand him, but too simple to know what
it was that Stavrogin asked of him.

Stavrogin had killed his own invincible
spirit, he had made the last trial of himself,
and had conquered—barrenness and desolation.
He was alone : there were not even any more
burdens that he might seek, no more battles
whose desperate prospect might fire his eyes.
He had won the final victory, and he was finally
alone. And in the pause and silence of his loneliness, he looks back upon the road he came
and he is afraid. He fears the grotesqueness
of it all—the outward act that is so mean and
ridiculous and shameful beside the inward intention. In the deathly calm of victory which
is his own defeat, he can hear the echo of some
far off malignant laughter, at the sordid shab-
biness of the things accomplished, which being
done were fraught with magnificent and eternal
issues. He had found in himself the courage

to ask life for an answer : for silence he had
steeled himself ; but the laughter in the silence
froze his heart. Against terror beyond the
physical he was strong, but before the obscenity
of timeless things he was afraid. Stavrogin is
haunted by that which has been called the
metaphysical obscenity, the devilish poverty
of the human thing beside the superhuman
intention ; and in his loneliness he is tortured
by the thought of " something shameful and
ridiculous." This same thought it is which
stays him from suicide. Mortal death can be
no more than a parody of the death which he
desires : he will not cheat himself again with
this last sham in an endless series of shams.
He cannot live, he cannot end his life. Nothing
remains.

Yet one thing does remain, the thought that
he may not be utterly alone. He who has
killed all instinct and all power to love in his
own soul, yet hungers to be loved. No man
will give him this, for no man understands
him ; but a woman may. She may know and
yet love ; and in the knowledge of that love, he
who knew that he could not love, might yet
lose the tyrant consciousness, and *be*. If a
woman should be found who should go open-
eyed to her doom in him, should know what
awaited her and yet make the sacrifice, then

he too might find in her salvation, and be born
anew by a belief in that which impelled her to
him. Stavrogin had made the attempt, he had
tried for love. *The Possessed* is strewn with
the bodies of the women whose life-blood he
had taken, and cast them away, —" ' Vampire
Stavrogin,' as a lady who loved him called
him." Shatov's wife and Shatov's sister had
been offered up upon his altar. But he had not
found in them that of which he stood in need,
and dreamed that he might obtain, not affection, nor sympathy nor tender care, nor any of
those things which a woman finds her life in
giving, but the sacrifice of life itself in love,
love that like himself " did not linger on the
brink, but in its desperation reached the pitch
of genius."

And when Lise came to him loving, knowing
herself unloved, there was the blinding moment
—a flash of hope kindled by a sudden and lovely
sacrifice, an hour's forgetfulness ; an hour that
quivered on the edge of happiness and expectation ; an hour taken in spite of all foreknow-
ledge that this would be like all the hours before
and end in barrenness ; an instant vision of a
soul and body beautifully given ; a momentary
ecstasy in the thought that he too might wholly
give, and take back a living self again, his old
soul mewed ; a spark of despairing hope that

all might yet be well with that soul sick unto
death ; one final challenge to his manifest
destiny.

I knew I did not love you, and yet I ruined you !
Yes, I accepted the moment for my own ; I had a
hope. . . . I've had it a long time . . . my last hope. . . .
I could not resist the radiance that flooded my heart
when you came to me yesterday, of yourself, alone,
of your own accord. I suddenly believed. . . . Perhaps
I have faith in it still.

One can hear those last words die away as
though they were frozen on his lips. Such
faith, faith in a miracle, were useless to him,
even if he had it : and he had it not. It was
only another possibility that he had dreamed.
For the wholly conscious mind there is no faith :
there is only that which is and that which
may be.

And Lise, because she saw and knew, was
the keenest eyed, as she is the most poignantly
beautiful of all Dostoevsky's women. "Ever
since those days in Switzerland I have had a
strong feeling that you have something awful,
loathsome, some bloodshed on your conscience
. . . and yet something that would make you
look ridiculous." If she knew so much and so
long, there was indeed no need of " the Operatic
Boat," and that was spoken in great bitterness of heart, when she too had come near to

feeling the vanity of all superhuman intention. But she had not known so much ever since those days in Switzerland ; she knew enough. She knew by instinct that Stavrogin had played high and greatly lost. Therefore she loved him. But the knowledge of the secret things, even that knowledge which compelled from her in horror : " God save me from your secrets," the knowledge of the something ridiculous, came surely to her in the unforgettable hour when they two were alone at Skvoreshniki, when for a moment Stavrogin believed, but the flame withered in his heart and dying withered hers. Such knowledge bought at such a price might well seem eternal and to have been before all things, and in the ocean of its age " ever since those days in Switzerland " to have been but a drop. For in that hour not love but life itself was dead.

Come, that's enough, that's enough. I am no good for anything and you're no good for anything ; it's as bad for both of us, so let's comfort ourselves with that. Anyway, it eases our vanity.

Lise was the only woman of them all who had the courage to enter the dark chamber of that heart. What she saw withered the soul within her as a moth's wings crumple and fall in a flame. She " burnt herself in a candle —

nothing more." She alone tried the depths. She put all her life into one mortal hour, and in it went to the place where was " the huge evil spider." " I have put all my life into one hour, and I am at peace," she said, because she was brave, to Nikolay Stavrogin, but when she had escaped from the web and the presence, and found herself in the arms of her earthly lover, her voice dropped timidly and she said : " I kept a bold face there all the time, but now I am afraid of death. I shall die soon, very soon, but I am afraid, I am afraid to die," for in the icy waste of Stavrogin's spirit she had seen that which lay beyond mortal life and death.

Stavrogin's last hope had failed as he knew it would fail ; he had now only to wait and endure to the end. Kirillov went to his death in the joy of delirium : Shatov's cruel end overtook him when he had just learnt what it was to be happy, in the presence of the miracle of the living life. *The Possessed* is a merciless book, but its victims neither ask nor receive our pity ; they know what awaits them, and they have our wonder, our sympathy and our admiration. But Shatov has our pity. He alone has touched the living life, " the mysterious coming of a new creature, a great and inexplicable mystery."

He needed to die, no doubt; but with his
death it is hardest of all to be reconciled. He
was at least worthy to meet his fate with his
eyes unbound. But, being such, his death is
Stavrogin's justification; it serves as yet
another pitiless reminder that it is the fact
of pain which drives Dostoevsky's spirits
" To strive, to seek, to find and not to
yield."

For Stavrogin is not a portent, but a possibility; he is mind with the courage of its own
knowledge. He has greater courage and insight than any of Dostoevsky's like characters,
and he has carried on the struggle of the individual will to heights far beyond theirs. The
logic of his life has never faltered; the last
tremor of the unconscious has been stilled
within him. Now he is wholly his own master,
and wholly rebellious to life; there are no more
traitor instincts in the camp. He is now "from
head to foot all marble constant," and he cannot deceive himself any more. He is Will, and
he has no desire to will; he has paid for victory
with his last breath of life. Therefore he does
not even desire to remain in the land of the
living, and he will not purchase the appearance
of reconciliation by suffering; besides, he cannot suffer any more. He has passed the last
torment of this life; all that he can hope for is

the miracle, the new consciousness, when there shall be no more time and the bodies of men shall be physically changed, and that, he knows, will " hardly be in our time." Death will bring no answer to his question, yet he cannot live on in the hope of a miracle which he knows will not be in his life, which yet must be in his life or it is only another sham. Still, it were better not to delude one's self with death.

So he sat down and wrote his letter to Darya Shatov. It is the final and complete confession of the defeat of consciousness.

DEAR DARYA PAVLOVNA,—At one time you expressed a wish to be my nurse, and made me promise to send for you when I wanted you. I am going away in two days and shall not come back. Will you go with me ?

Last year, like Herzen, I was naturalised as a citizen of the canton of Uri, and that nobody knows. There I've already bought a little house. I've still twelve thousand roubles left ; we'll go and live there for ever. I don't want to go anywhere else ever.

It's a very dull place, a narrow valley, the mountains restrict both vision and thought. It's very gloomy. I chose the place because there was a little house to be sold. If you don't like it I'll sell it and buy another in some other place.

FYODOR DOSTOEVSKY

I am not well, but I hope to get rid of hallucinations in that air. It's physical, and as for the moral you know everything ; but do you know all ?

I've told you a great deal of my life but not all. Even to you ! Not all. By the way, I repeat that in my conscience I feel myself responsible for my wife's death. I haven't seen you since then, that's why I repeat it. I feel guilty about Lizaveta Nikolaevna too ; but you know about that ; you foretold almost all that.

Better not come to me. My asking you is a horrible meanness. And why should you bury your life with me ? You are dear to me, and when I was miserable it was good to be beside you ; only with you could I speak of myself aloud. But that proves nothing. You defined it yourself, " a nurse "—it's your own expression ; why sacrifice so much ? Grasp this, too, that I have no pity for you since I ask you, and no respect for you since I reckon on you. And yet I ask you and I reckon on you. In any case I need your answer for I must set off very soon. In that case I shall go alone.

I expect nothing of Uri ; I am simply going. I have not chosen a gloomy place on purpose. I have no ties in Russia—everything is as alien to me there as everywhere. It's true that I dislike living there more than anywhere ; but I can't hate anything even there !

I've tried my strength everywhere. You advised me to do this " that I might learn to know myself." As long I was experimenting for myself and for others it seemed infinite, as it has all my life. Before your eyes I endured a blow from your brother ; I acknowledged

192

my marriage in public. But to what to apply my strength, that is what I've never seen and do not see now in spite of all your praises in Switzerland, which I believed in. I am still capable as I always was of desiring to do something good and of feeling pleasure from it ; at the same time I desire evil and feel pleasure from that too. But both feelings are always too petty, and are never very strong. My desires are too weak ; they are not enough to guide me. On a log one may cross a river, but not on a chip. I say this that you may not believe that I am going to Uri with hopes of any sort.

As always I blame no one. I've tried the depths of debauchery and wasted my strength over it. But I don't like vice and didn't want it. You have been watching me of late. Do you know that I looked upon our iconoclasts with spite, from envy of their hopes ? But you had no need to be afraid. I could not have been one of them for I never shared anything with them. And to do it for fun, from spite I could not either, not because I am afraid of the ridiculous—I cannot be afraid of the ridiculous—but because I have, after all, the habits of a gentleman and it disgusted me. But if I had felt more spite and envy of them I might perhaps have joined them. You can judge how hard it has been for me, and how I've struggled from one thing to another.

Dear friend ! Great and tender heart which I divined ! Perhaps you dream of giving me so much love and lavishing on me so much that is beautiful from your beautiful soul, that you hope to set up some aim for me at last by it ? No, it's better for you to be more cautious, my love will be as petty as I am myself and you will be unhappy. Your brother told me that the man who loses connection with his country loses his gods, that is, all his aims. One may argue about everything endlessly, but from me nothing has come but negation, with no greatness of soul, no force. Even negation has not come from me. Everything has always been petty and spiritless. Kirillov in the greatness of his soul could not compromise with an idea and shot himself; but I see, of course, that he was great-souled, because he had lost his reason. I can never lose my reason, and I can never believe in an idea to such a degree as he did. I cannot even be interested in an idea to such a degree. I can never, never shoot myself.

I know I ought to kill myself, to brush myself off the earth like a nasty insect; but I am afraid of suicide, for I am afraid of showing greatness of soul. I know that it will be another sham again—the last deception in an endless series of deceptions. What good is there in deceiving one's self. Simply to play at greatness of soul ? Indignation and shame I can never feel therefore not despair.

Forgive me for writing so much. I wrote without noticing. A hundred pages would be too little and ten lines would be enough. Ten lines would be enough to ask you to be a nurse. Since I left Skvoreshniki I've been living at the sixth station on the line at the stationmaster's. I got to know him in the time of debauchery five years ago in Petersburg. No one knows I am living there. Write to him. I enclose the address.

NIKOLAY STAVROGIN.

THE POSSESSED

" A hundred pages would be too little and ten lines would be enough." Stavrogin said his say in even less than ten lines ; he said it without even opening his lips. Now, he was not any more afraid of the ridiculous, and he could face the terror of metaphysical obscenity as he had faced all other things. He could even smile at it and indulge it. I do not know if I am in this differently constituted to other readers of Dostoevsky ; but of all the cruel and terrible things in his books that which haunts me most is the vision of Stavrogin's suicide.

The citizen of the canton of Uri was hanging there behind the door. On the table lay a piece of paper with the words in pencil : " No one is to blame. I did it myself." Beside it on the table lay a hammer, a piece of soap and a large nail—obviously an extra one in case of need. The strong silk cord upon which Nikolay Vsyevolodovitch had hanged himself had evidently been chosen and prepared beforehand and was thickly smeared with soap.

What is most terrible is that piece of soap. He, who was after all too much of a gentleman to hang himself in a noose less delicate than one of silk, had almost deceived himself at the last with the elegance of his act of destruction. Perhaps the last instinct of all was one that he could not have foreknown, the instinct of the

aristocrat to die finely. This too he crushed.
I do not like to think of the cold and bitter
smile with which he remembered a piece of
soap. A silk cord runs easily without such aids.
But while he smeared the noose thickly, he had
won another victory. He had himself parodied
his own determination ; he had taken thought
at the last that he should not show greatness
of soul nor leave the name of one who had
shown it. With his piece of soap he had anticipated the last obscenity of things.

With Stavrogin's death the last hope of consciousness and conscious will is gone. The
most splendid of all the Possessed has rushed
down the steep into the sea ; rather he has not
rushed, but he has gone delicately, like the
prince he was, and held himself proof against
even the ecstasy of self-destruction. And he
is the Prince of this world, for it is not certain
proud spirits, but all an age, an epoch of the
human consciousness that is possessed. Dostoevsky lavished himself upon the creation of
Stavrogin. If Shatov and Kirillov saw in him
their God and Pyotr Verhovensky divined in
him the prince of the world which should be
built up on the ruins of the old, it was not because they were blind, but because he was in
very truth the man-God and the prince. Dostoevsky knew that he was the perfect embodi-

ment of an age, superhuman only because he had all the courage of his humanity. Yet he was possessed. Life cannot end in barrenness and destruction, yet it can have no other end. The old life—and it is this old life in which we live to-day—came to its perfect and inhuman flower in Stavrogin; but, because this cannot be the end, a miracle *must* be at hand. It was left to Stepan Verhovensky to read the parable.

" My friend," said Stepan Trofimovitch in great excitement, " *savez-vous* that wonderful and . . . extraordinary passage has been a stumbling-block to me all my life . . . *dans ce livre* . . . so much so that I remembered those verses from childhood. Now an idea has occurred to me ; *une comparaison.* A great number of ideas keep coming into my mind now. You see that's exactly like our Russia, those devils that come out of the sick man and enter into the swine. They are all the sores, all the foul contagions, all the impurities, all the devils great and small that have multiplied in that great invalid, our beloved Russia, in the course of ages and ages. *Oui, cette Russie que j'aimais toujours.* But a great idea and a great Will will encompass it from on high, as with that lunatic possessed of devils . . . and all those devils will come forth, all the impurity, all the rottenness that was putrefying on the surface . . . and they will beg of themselves to enter into swine : and indeed maybe they have entered into them already ! They are we, we and those . . . and Petrusha and *les autres avec lui* . . . and I perhaps at the head of them, and we shall cast ourselves down, possessed and raving, from the rocks into the sea, and we shall all be drowned—and a good thing too, for that is all we are fit for. But the sick man will be healed and ' will sit at the feet of Jesus,' and all will look upon him with astonishment. . . . My dear, *vous comprendrez après*, but now it excites me very much . . . *Vous comprendrez après. Nous comprendrons ensemble.*"

From out of the desolation and sickness must arise a new life of which the man clothed and in his right mind is the symbol. But the sickness is a sickness unto universal death, for it is the human consciousness itself which is the disease. It is a manifestation of life which destroys life. In Stavrogin Dostoevsky had sent forth the greatest of its champions, and he had been vanquished. There remained only the new man, clothed and in his right mind, for a hope. In the new man must be found the new consciousness ; in him the assurance of eternal harmony which came to the old man only in the delirium of his sickness, shall be part of his waking knowledge.

It may be that this hope will seem to some a fantastic and unintelligible dream. The logician will say that the destruction of the present human consciousness and the creation of a new life, wherein spirit shall be no longer divided from body, is no more than empty words which correspond to no thought : the thought in them, they will say, is unthinkable. It is true ; yet on the foundation of such unthinkable thoughts Dostoevsky's great work is builded. Those who are not prepared to think them have no business with his books ; they will consider his novels to be merely novels, his truth to be merely truth, and his art to be merely art. They should remain within their own garden and enjoy its fruits, which are by no means uncomely ; they have the hither to elect upon their side. Even among the Russians they have with them Turgeniev, who saw only a digger of psychological mole-runs or a Marquis de Sade in Dostoevsky, and Tolstoi, who could say that he had no intellect. Turgeniev was a novelist ; Tolstoi was a great novelist ; Dostoevsky was not a novelist at all. He cannot be measured by the old art or the old logic ; he transcended both.

" Transcended " is a hard word, which can be too easily used ; yet it contains the truth of Dostoevsky's art and thought. His art was the way of escape from his tormenting doubts, the means of expression for his unthinkable thoughts. The present consciousness he strained to its uttermost limits. Its forms of art and thought he tortured and loaded till they could bear the burden no longer, as his

own body could not support the agonised
strivings of his spirit. He had somehow to
express within these forms visions and ideas
which passed beyond them. He deliberately
poured a new wine into the old bottles knowing
that they would burst ; and in himself he felt
the incessant ferment of conceptions which it
passed even his power to make vocal. The old
expressions he charged with a content that was
fantastical ; his Christianity is not Christianity,
his realism is not realism, his novels are not
novels, his truth not truth, his art not art.
His world is a world of symbols and potentialities which are emboded in unlivable lives ;
for the art and the creative activity which was
the only way of escape from the unendurable
torments of his mind, had perforce to be com-
mensurate with the doubts which were the
cause of the torments. Therefore his art was
metaphysical, which no art can be. He
struggled to express conceptions which were
truly inexpressible, for which he had need not
only of a new art but of a new philosophy. In
part he created both these things ; he was at
least " the prophetic soul of the wide world
dreaming on things to come," and he strove
to communicate his visions by the instrument
of a language and thought that could hardly
contain them, as Kirillov's broken and mysteri-

ous speech seems like the translation of a fragment of a known, yet ineffable whole, into words which enfeeble and denature it. In one of his last letters Dostoevsky refers to a sentence of Vladimir Solovyev, the Russian philosopher, who in his youth was surely Dostoevsky's disciple : " I am firmly convinced that mankind *knows much more* than it has hitherto expressed either in philosophy or art." " Just so it is with me," Dostoevsky adds. It was Vladimir Solovyev who used to call Dostoevsky a prophet : and a prophet he was, not in the vulgar sense of one who professes to foretell the incessant changes in the configuration of the material world, but of one who contemplated and sought to penetrate into a new consciousness and a new mode of being which he saw was metaphysically inevitable for mankind.

Dostoevsky stands upon the furthest edge of the old, which is the threshold of the new. In Stavrogin he had gone his lonely way to the ultimate outpost of the present Dispensation. One task fronted him now, to create, if he could, the miracle, and to step forward by one great and despairing effort across the chasm which divides that which is from that which is to come. He paused for long to gather all his strength for the *salto mortale*. That which he wrote between *The Possessed* and *The Brothers Karamazov* is no more than an episode, a breathing space in the life-long struggle. *A Raw Youth*, which is a brilliant study in the adolescent consciousness of a nation which has in a hundred years lived through an eternity of the spirit, and *The Journal of an Author*, are only the constant exercise in arms of one preparing for the final onset, which is *The Brothers Karamazov*. In that crowning effort death overtook him.

THE BROTHERS KARAMAZOV

NEARLY ten years' study and thought went to the making of *The Brothers Karamazov*. The book has been called " an encyclopædia of Russian life," rather, I suppose, to convey its comprehensiveness than to define its character ; for the name is a foolish one. Dostoevsky could not write an encyclopædia ; he could not represent life, and it is certain that, considered as a picture of Russian life, *The Brothers Karamazov* is fundamentally false. In this work, above all others, Dostoevsky deliberately annihilated all sense of time. The events of the one day which occupies one half the book resist all efforts at enclosure within our human computation, and there can be no doubt in the mind prepared to accept Dostoevsky for what he is, that whether his intention be conscious or unconscious he bears us away at the very opening of the story into the timeless world of spirit.

There are events, enthralling happenings,

through whose material agency the drama of the spirit is unfolded, for the agonists are potencies of the human soul. Nor are they merely potencies ; that which is possible for the human spirit is its ultimate reality. But to bring these possibilities together into one time, one space, one family, is to load the lesser reality in which we live beyond its endurance. Yet this is what Dostoevsky did in *The Brothers Karamazov*. Two women and five men are the persons of the drama : the father, Fyodor, the three legitimate sons, Dmitri, Ivan, and Alyosha, his natural son, Smerdyakov, and Grushenka and Katerina Ivanovna. Of these the women play their part wholly in the material or earthly history. They are necessary to the events which happen in time, and in some sort the medium by whose aid the spirits of the men are made incarnate. On Fyodor's struggle with Dmitri for the possession of Grushenka the narrative is built ; but this awful contest is in its deep intention not for the prize of Grushenka's body, but rooted in the natural hostility of the father and the son. It is not an accident of their desiring the same bodily beauty which sets them in opposition ; they are enemies one to the other, since time began. Likewise it is with Dmitri and Ivan and Katerina Ivanovna. Ivan hates Dmitri, not because he is preferred in Katerina Ivanovna's love, but because it is in his destiny to hate his brother. We are aware of these things, even though we do not know them, when we first read the book in which they are written. The violence and terror of the passions which are unloosed in these men is beyond their earthly object. We can devise a hundred ways for averting the *actual* horror of that murder; but intuitively we know that the father must be slain. His death is not ordained by any individual will, but by the spirit of man. He belongs to the darkness which is past, like an obscene beast evoked out of another time. Man has passed beyond him, and if he bursts out of the oblivion which is his rightful prison, then he must die.

Yet wherein is his offence? He is a sensualist; but his sons are sensualists. We do not hate Ivan and Dmitri. They are with us; they loathe and hate their father, yet they are of his blood, and his spirit is them. They know they are like him, and it is for that they hate and fear him. As the father is to us, so is he to them; he is their very substance, that in them which being tamed is their being, and being unconquered, their death. They have put their father away from them, yet are they haunted by the fear that they may be like him ; they long to deny him as their begetter, yet they know that they are part of him. He is their past, his spirit has been in them fashioned anew. There is a profound difference between him and them, yet, when they look upon him, they are afraid that the difference may be as nothing, and the identity every-thing ; and they are terrified by their own tormenting conviction that the new form of the old being may be no more than a flimsy veneer.

Perhaps the veneer is flimsy enough. All that divides them from him is their conscious-ness. He is the beast, yet he does not know himself for the beast ; if he had this know-ledge he would be other than he is, and his great strength would be weakened. It seems that he has no other conception of his own foulness than that which comes to him from the loath-ing and disgust in the faces of those with whom he speaks. When he tells to Ivan and Alyosha the revolting story of his devilish cruelty to their mother he is absolutely insensible to its effect upon them ; he is amazed that Alyosha should burst into a paroxysm of sudden, violent, silent weeping, while, so far from an-ticipating Ivan's anger and contempt, he has utterly forgotten that Alyosha's mother was Ivan's mother also. He is cunning and cruel

and foul, but he is also less than human. He
seems to work his wickedness not deliberately,
and in some sense not to be accountable for his
foulness, as though Dostoevsky the sorcerer,
like Prospero in the magic isle, had endued
this Caliban with words which had for him no
inward meaning :

Abhorred slave,
Which any print of goodness will not take,
Being capable of all ill. I pitied thee,
Took pains to make thee speak, taught thee each hour
One thing or other : when thou didst not, savage,
Know thine own meaning, but wouldst gabble like
A thing most brutish, I endowed thy purposes
With words that made them known : but thy vile
    race,
Though thou didst learn, had that in't which good
    natures
Could not abide to be with. . . .

Not good natures only, but human nature
itself, which has in the ages become conscious,
cannot abide to be with Fyodor Pavlovitch.
Words do not belong to him by right, but by
some black art he has been clothed with the
prerogatives of humanity, and from beneath
their disguise there shows something which
rouses a shudder of physical repulsion in his
sons, who know themselves to be insecurely
set at one precarious remove from his condition. " Perhaps I shan't kill him," says

207

Dmitri, " and perhaps I shall. I'm afraid that he will suddenly become so loathsome to me with his face at that moment. I hate his ugly throat, his nose, his eyes, his shameless snigger. I feel a physical repulsion. That's what I'm afraid of. That's what may be too much for me." And Ivan has but one word for him : the pig. With a cunning irony the old man indulges the thought and retorts upon them : " Ah, you boys ! You children, little sucking pigs. . . ."

Of the little sucking pigs, Ivan and Dmitri stand together. The father knows that these are his enemies, and though he fears the bodily violence of Dmitri in his anger, he is still more afraid of Ivan ; for Ivan is clairvoyant, and he from deliberate reasoning may do that to which Dmitri can be impelled only by a sudden access of consuming anger. The hatred and contempt of Ivan for his father is fixed and irrevocable, because it is in essence an intellectual passion. " Fyodor Pavlovitch, our papa, was a pig," says Ivan to Dmitri when he is in prison, " but his ideas were right enough " ; and it is precisely because his ideas are right enough, and the final issue of all Ivan's impassioned dialectic is embodied in this pig, that Ivan detests him. Fyodor Pavlovitch is the swine of the Temptation of St. Antony, teh jeer of eternity at the human spirit which consumes itself in the fires of its passion for knowledge, and in him Ivan has always before him the vision of the man which was, by the mere fact of his being, paralysing the man which is by the revelation of his ultimate impotence. His father is that which his mind tells him he must be, and yet he cannot be : and Ivan hates him steadfastly for his power. Fyodor Pavlovitch *is* something ; Ivan is nothing at all. He is tempest-tossed between his two desires, to love life and to know the meaning of it, and his soul is ill-compact of instincts which he cannot justify and seekings which end in nothingness, while beneath the impotent frenzy of his tormented brain slumbers the conviction that all his doubts and demands may be illusion and vanity, and no more than the thin garment which covers for a little while within him the dark beast of the father's soul.

He is nearer to his father than is Dmitri, for all the wide space that separates them to the eye. He is complex, while Dmitri is simple. He can approve his father, which Dmitri could never do ; and he feels the presence of his father's soul within him. The instinctive and overwhelming physical repulsion which sweeps over Dmitri when he stands before Fyodor Pavlovitch, is denied to Ivan, whose mind but not his being abhors his father, for in him he recognises a power which is its own justification, and a kinship which goes deeper than conscious denial. Ivan knows that the spirit of the father is the thirst for life. " We shall meet before I am thirty," he says to Alyosha, " when I shall begin to want to turn aside from the cup. Father doesn't want to turn aside from his cup till he is seventy, he dreams of hanging on to eighty, so he says. He means it only too seriously, though he is a buffoon. He stands upon a firm rock, too, he stands upon his sensuality—though after we are thirty indeed there may be nothing else to stand on. . . . But to hang on to seventy is nasty, better only to thirty ; one might retain ' a shadow of nobility ' by deceiving one's self. . . ." In such a moment Ivan is forced to confess that the difference between them is precariously based in the son's desire to retain " a shadow of nobility," some reflection of the youthful days in which the thirst for life had not been narrowed, by the eventual barrenness of all loftier search, to the perpetual quest for sensual gratification. If that is all that remains of the high hopes and the strength of youth thirsting for life, loving the meaning of life no less than life itself (of which the aspirations of conscious-ness are not the least part), then to hang on to seventy is nasty. But this, Ivan knows, is a declaration made in the heady nobility of youth ; there may at thirty indeed be nothing else to stand on. . . .

Beside the intellectual complexity of Ivan, which for all his youth soars at times to cold and dizzy heights of speculation, Dmitri's simplicity is transparent. On the night when he has taken the fatal decision and torn the little bag from his neck, while he is driving furiously to Mokroe and Grushenka, Andrey the coachman turns round to him and says : " But you're like a little child—that's how we look on you." And he has the naïveté of a child. He sins in simpleness of heart, conscious and repentant of his own waywardness. He is violent, passionate and dissipated ; and withal generous and honest. Though he says that he has thought much about passion, his thinking is not so much the work of the mind as of instinct. By instinct he seeks for some repose either in the passion of love or in a simple faith. " The awful thing," he says to Alyosha, " is that beauty is mysterious. God and the devil are fighting there, and the battlefield is the heart of man." His contrary instincts he can neither question nor justify : intuition, not intellect, guides him, so that he can accept with a childish faith the arguments of Ivan for

gospel, and revere their author for an oracle ;
yet he will never act by the argument he has
adopted. Even a shallow cunning fool like
Rakitin, the monk who turns journalist, has
logic enough to deceive Dmitri's brain. But
in spite of all intellectual deceptions he holds
fast by his own nature ; he does nothing
deliberately, but all things by impulse, yet he
does not wholly trust his impulse or his intuition, for, being conscious of the war within his
own heart, he is ready to abase himself before
the imaginary perfections of others. He knows
that Katerina Ivanovna does not love him, as
well as Ivan knows it, and even though he cannot explain it so clearly as his brother he knows
that she is a monster of pride, in love with her
own virtue, pursuing him with her magnan-
imity, although she has hated him ever since
their first meeting for the blow he dealt her
self-esteem ; and yet, in spite of his inward
conviction, he is prepared to assure himself that
she is a perfect being, and he himself in her regard a devil of baseness and ingratitude. Even
when he has finally broken with her, and
written the incriminating letter which she uses
to ruin him : " He murdered his father and
ruined himself to hold his ground rather than
endure your pride . . . And he doesn't love you :
Your slave and enemy," she is still upon his

conscience. In prison the thought of her tortures him, and he is profoundly miserable until he shall receive her forgiveness, which she refuses him. He is, in truth, the simple-hearted Mitka, who towards others is always an idealist and towards himself a merciless and unfair judge.

For Dmitri too is a seeker. Though he is a physical and ungovernable man, he has the vision of some harmony and beauty which he may attain through the body. He cannot deny the body, neither can be find rest in it, and he gropes blindly after the secret and mystery of repose. As Ivan is a mind, through which he feels the insurgent body will rise and overthrow the stronghold of his consciousness, so Dmitri is a body amongst whose tumultuous and absorbing life mind like an insidious ferment works its way. " You see," he says to Alyosha in prison, " I never had any of these doubts before, but it was hidden away in me. It was perhaps just because ideas I did not understand were surging up in me that I used to drink and fight and rage. It was to stifle them in myself, to still them, to smother them." And the new doubt that has climbed its painful way through the recesses of his being into the mind's daylight is that incessant question : " What if He doesn't exist ? " What if everything should

be lawful, and the harmony in which he had in
spite of all placed an instinctive and unreasoning trust be only an empty dream ? Dmitri is
sorry to lose God, for God was a means of
repose, and without Him he has only the consciousness that he must find rest and the knowledge that the way to it is hidden from him.
So Dmitri, the body, turned to Ivan, the mind,
seeking for guidance, and desiring to drink from
the springs of his soul : and Ivan was silent as
the tomb. Once only did Ivan vouchsafe him
a word, which was terrible : " Fyodor Pavlovitch, our papa, was a pig ; but his ideas were
right enough." To Dmitri that was worse than
Rakitin. It was better to have a bare denial of
all harmony and purpose than that his father
should be approved. If there was nothing, it
were better to know and face the desolation
than to believe that the swinishness of the old
man was right, for this at least Dmitri could
not but abhor. He was a sensualist, too, but
he knew himself for what he was, and he
sought for that which must lie beyond it. " I
go on and I don't know whether I'm going to
shame or to light and joy." But the hope of
the light and the joy sustained him ; he strove
for a consummation that should be worthy of
his humanity. The darkness of the beast was
put behind him ; he was at least a man.

And Dmitri's love for Grushenka, upon which the real or earthly story turns, is the passionate love of a man for a woman. He may talk about the Karamazov "bug" which creeps about within him and spreads the plague of baseness in his soul, but it is only the language of self-abasement. His passion for Grushenka is the desire of one fierce and simple heart for another. She, like him, deceives herself with the imaginary perfections of others. Love is the whole of life to her; and for love she will sacrifice everything, and even disregard the promptings of her intuition in the ardour of her desire to believe in it. She can crush the certainty of her conviction of his worthlessness in order to believe in the Polish lover who deserted her; and for five years she can remain faithful to the man of her imagination, because, having given him all, she cannot but believe that he is in return wholly hers. If she were to lose her faith in the all-sufficiency of love, nothing would be left her. She is jealous and strong and true; she can deceive herself for the sake of her faith in love, but another's pretence of love cannot deceive her. Her intuition sees clearly into the nature of Katerina Ivanovna, when she will not kiss her hand, and she strikes back ruthlessly, because she cannot "be won over with chocolate," and resents the blind contempt and pride of Katerina's approach to her. Even then she loves Dmitri's noble heart, and were there not an older loyalty to contend with her new love, she would have been wholly his, for their simple, jealous, fierce natures are destined for each other. But she cannot root her first love out of her heart, and when the message comes for her to go to Mokroe, her loyalty and faith in love magnificently triumphs over her contempt for her own much endurance.

" He has sent for me," she cried, her face white and distorted with a wan smile : " he whistles ! Crawl back, little dog ! "
But only for one instant she stood as though hesitating ; suddenly the blood rushed to her head and sent a glow to her cheeks !
" I will go," she cried ; " five years of my life ! Good-bye ! Good-bye, Alyosha, my fate is sealed. Go, go, leave me, all of you, don't let me see you again. Grushenka is flying to a new life. . . . Don't you remember evil against me either, Rakitin. I may be going to my death ! Ugh ! I feel as though I were drunk ! "

Grushenka, too, is stayed by the hope of the new life which will be found in love. The love of which she dreams is beyond the body yet through the body.

Nevertheless, though in her and in Dmitri's

infatuation for her Dostoevsky reached the
most perfect expression of passionate love that
is to be found in all his work, Grushenka has
no part in the timeless drama which is the inner
reality of *The Brothers Karamazov*. She is in
its comparison no more than a twig borne along
by the rushing torrent of the Karamazov
spirit. Katerina Ivanovna, Father Zossima
himself are no more than this. The father and
the sons are set apart from the world, and they
are conscious of their separation. Each one
of them recognises at some period of the story
that a power works in him, which is of another
kind than human impulse. Alyosha asks himself : Does the spirit of God move over that
spirit ? and he must confess that he does not
know. It is too big to be thus limited, for within itself it contains both good and evil. The
Karamazov spirit is older than good and evil
themselves.

What then is this mighty spirit that is manifested in Fyodor and Dmitri and Ivan and
Alyosha ? Heredity explains nothing, for it
tells us nothing of what the heirs inherit. And
this thing is not sensualism. Neither Ivan nor
Alyosha are within any human meaning of the
word sensualists. Sensualism is but one single
form of a mightier power. Nor is it a passionate
thirst for life. All men have this in their

degree, and it is not enough to say that the Karamazovs have merely a greater thirst for life than their fellows. They are divided absolutely from mankind. In so far as they are like men, the spirit which moves them must be described in human and relative terms. But they too are spirits ; they are not men with a passionate thirst for life, they are Life itself, and in the generations of the Karamazov family not human lives but epochs of the human consciousness are born and die.

In this book Dostoevsky gathered together all the thought, the doubt, and the faith of a lifetime, into one timeless survey of life itself. To see less than this in *The Brothers Karamazov* is to be condemned to see nothing but a chaos illumined by fitful flashes of genius. There is no chaos in Dostoevsky's work. Its strangeness is due to the immensity of its form. And if the categorical statement that the Karamazov family represents life itself seen by the eye of genius *sub specie aeternitatis* is too abrupt, in spite of the endeavour that has been made to show the process of his vision to this necessary and final culmination, then we have only to follow out the clue that is afforded by the recurrence in *The Brothers Karamazov* of figures whose significance has already been established.

Ivan Karamazov belongs to the order of

Stavrogin and Svidrigailov ; but in him the conception has been made yet more abstract. He is, as it were, the mind of Stavrogin apart from the body. He has no past of attempted action behind him ; he is only a consciousness which has brooded over the destiny of mankind. In him the seeking mind is borne onwards to what seems like a delirium of abstract speculation. The profound thought which underlies " The Grand Inquisitor " is simplicity itself compared with the torments which he suffers from his own mind in the Dream. Nothing has ever been written like that Dream ; it is saturated with the metaphysical terror and obscenity which is the appointed end of the striving of the human consciousness. In Ivan the road of this perilous progress is made clearer than in any other of Dostoevsky's characters. In the tavern he reveals himself to Alyosha : —

... And so I accept God and am glad to, and what's more I accept His wisdom, His purpose—which are utterly beyond our ken ; I believe in the underlying order and the meaning of life ; I believe in the eternal harmony in which they say we shall one day be blended. I believe in the Word to which the universe is striving, and Which Itself was " with God," and Which Itself is God, and so on, and so on, to infinity. There are all sorts of phrases for it. I seem to be on the right path, don't I ? Yet would you believe it, in the final result I don't accept this world of God's, and although I know it exists I don't accept it at all. It's not that I don't accept God, you must understand, it's the world created by Him I don't and cannot accept. Let me make it plain. I believe like a child that suffering will be healed and made up for, that all the humiliating absurdity of human contradictions will vanish like a pitiful mirage, like the despicable fabrication of the impotent and infinitely small Euclidean mind of man, that in the world's finale, at the moment of eternal harmony, something so precious will come to pass that it will suffice for all hearts, for the comforting of all resentments, for the atonement of all the crimes of humanity, of all the blood they've shed ; that it will make it not only possible to forgive but to justify all that has happened with men—but though all that may come to pass, I don't accept it. I won't accept it. . . .

And when he has explained why he will not accept harmony at the price of suffering and pain, he continues : —

I don't want harmony. From love to humanity I don't want it. I would rather be left with the unavenged suffering. I would rather remain with my unavenged suffering and my unsatisfied indignation, *even if I were wrong*. Besides, too high a price is asked for harmony ; it's beyond our means to pay so much to enter on it. And so I hasten to give back my entrance ticket, and if I am an honest man I am bound to give it back as soon as possible. And that I am doing. It's not God that I don't accept, Alyosha, only I most respectfully return Him the ticket. . . .

" One can hardly live in rebellion, and I want to live." It is hardly possible to hand back the ticket, by no means so simple a matter, anyhow, as putting a bullet through one's brain. An Ivan knows that the act of self-destruction is like spinning a coin : heads, more of this mockery called life ; tails, real death. Poor devils ! if it were a real coin with heads on one side and tails on the other, perhaps they would be happier. A good, sound, even chance of final annihilation might comfort them. But these vague whispers of eternal harmony, these misty surmises of some ineffable beatitude wherein they might see that all is good and the voice of approbation be compelled from them, these it is which fill them with cold desolation. To praise the creator of this world—if the chance were but one in a million of such a consummation, how bitter is the poison on their lips !

And in the " Dream " the *salto mortale* has been taken. Ivan stands on the thither side of mortality. He has spun the coin ; and he has lost the toss. " All that you have, we have," says the Devil, " even old ladies of eighteen stone and the stings of conscience for punishment." The desolate vista of æon on æon, eternity opening out on to yet another eternity, is revealed, but not the secret. " They won't tell me the secret, because I might bawl Hosanna and the indispensable minus would disappear." This devil in the seedy frock-coat and the out-of-date eyeglass would indisputably bawl, for he is the symbol of a possibility, and in the clear, cold air of the rebellious mind, the possible is the truly real. It would be something, would it not, if these tortured rebel souls could know that evil was a mighty power, magnificent in its strength and noble in its deliberate blackness, which they might serve or fight and be in either unashamed. It would be something to have finally laid the ghost of harmony. But the odds are that it does exist, and then what if evil should be something sordid and vulgar, some seedy down at heels purpose, pitched by the unknown into a mechanical occupation, a short-sighted clerk doing his duty every day over the ledger without ever a spark of knowledge of the end that his activity served ? There is not much room for romanticism when you have grown used to the idea of eternity. " How can such a vulgar devil visit such a great man as you ? "

It is a bitter thought, but not so bitter as that other doubt, that this devil has nothing new, that he is no more than the vulgar and stupid part of Ivan. If he were only vulgar and stupid in his own right, if he only corporeally and indisputably *was*, then in that knowledge Ivan might find rest. Let him be vulgar, be stupid, be low, even let him carry a tail like a great Dane, only let him *be*. Let him be anything rather than the imagination of Ivan's own brain. This modern Hamlet craves for a *being*, not for principalities and powers any more — those dreams have gone the way of the old heroisms — but just for a being. It would be even comfortable to have a being who shared his thoughts, a being with the same doubts and the same horror (even though being seedy and bourgeois he should choose the high-sounding name of " æsthetic " for his repulsion) of being compelled to shout Hosanna ! But in that realm of indeterminate equations there is hardly a chance of falling among friends, even if the friend should prove only to be a poor relation. Svidrigailov's conjecture is a likelier one.

Ivan has gone far on the way of consciousness, farther perhaps than any before him, and he stands fainting at the end of the cul-de-sac. He has thought of the man-God ; but his mind will not suffer so gross a deception. Before the mind of the man-God will remain the same vast unknown. When all human science has been taken to the farthest edge of the knowable, nothing has been accomplished for the soul which craves for being. These minds are not deceived; when all their feverish dreams of being beyond their own have fled away, and they are alone, then comes another question, whether they themselves are. Being pitifully honest minds they answer that they have no assurance of anything save their own will to be, for even they are not. The *cogito ergo sum* is not sufficient any more. Their dialectic goes deeper than that of the good Monsieur Descartes. Their *volo esse quia cogito* is a slenderer foundation on which to build, when they have learnt that beneath that consciousness and that conscious will lie things that will not ever come under its domination, things in comparison with which the daylight of the knowing, willing mind itself may be no more than a dream. It is indeed always worth while to talk to a clever man, and when Smerdyakov tells Ivan that he has his father's soul, Ivan must admit that he has not wasted his time.

" You are like Fyodor Pavlovitch, you are more like him than any of his children ; you've the same soul as he had."

" You are not a fool," said Ivan, seeming struck. The blood rushed to his face. " You are serious now ! " he observed, looking suddenly at Smerdyakov with a different expression. " It was your pride," answered Smerdyakov, " made you think I was a fool.'

The human consciousness is proud, and though man cannot live in rebellion, yet since rebellion must be, the mind can only be maintained by the pride of its rebellion. But what if it cannot rebel, and the proud will to be itself be only a waking dream ?

And even in his waking moments, Ivan is not spared. The Devil for the time of dreams, and Smerdyakov for the daylight, are his familiars. The two truths are living and abroad. Hamlet had pondered what dreams may come in that sleep of death ; but Ivan had a double burden, those old dreams, and these others that haunt this sleep of life ; and it was a little harder to tell Smerdyakov that he was Ivan's dream. He could not be scared by an inkstand or a glass. Smerdyakov, who made love to Marfa, sang in a sweet and sugary voice sentimental songs to the guitar, discussed God with poor old Grigory, was not a ghost to be laid. His hair oil, his polished glacé boots, his French exercise books and his admirable soups, had all too deep a savour of the concrete and the real to be dispelled by a movement of the brain. Alyosha, who could not see the Devil, could see Smerdyakov ; and probably Smerdyakov was less pleasant of the two to behold. The Devil, who was clever enough to throw doubt upon his own reality, had not enough metaphysics to discredit Ivan's own. On the contrary, he professed a certain envious preference for the realism of earth " where all is formulated and geometrical," advantages of a condition which Ivan at least shared. Of course, it may have been that when he was tired of being a shabby-genteel Russian gentleman *qui faisait la cin-quantaine,* he chose to incarnate himself in the valet, and it is, moreover, certain that he made his one recorded appearance in his proper person, at the moment that Smerdyakov had given up the ghost. But whether Smerdyakov were really he or not, is a question of little moment : they were all closely related, and in any case Ivan found Smerdyakov the more tormenting of the two. For the existence of Smerdyakov was a direct challenge to Ivan's own. If he was not the Devil, at least they both had learned the precise trick of obtruding upon his consciousness in the same school.

Sitting down again, Ivan began looking round as though searching for something. This happened several times. At last his eyes were fastened intently upon one point. Ivan smiled, but an angry flush suffused his face. He sat a long while in his place, his head propped on both arms, though he looked sideways at the same point, at the sofa which stood against the opposite wall. There was evidently something, some object that irritated him there, worried and tormented him. . . .

That was one of them. Here is the other.

Ivan tried not to think, but that, too, was no use.
What made his depression so vexatious and irritating
was that it had a kind of casual, external character—
he felt that. Some person or thing seemed to be standing out somewhere, just as something will sometimes
obtrude itself on the eye, and though one may be so
busy that for a long time one does not notice it, yet
it irritates and almost torments one, till at last one
realises, and removes the offending object. . . .

It would be hard to distinguish the one
from the other by anything in his manner of
announcing himself, though, as a matter of
history, the former was the Devil and the latter
Smerdyakov. For they are both " poor relations," with the same irritating trick of waiting
till they are noticed, the same insistent defer-
ence of holding their peace until they are
spoken to, and beneath it all the same revolting
familiarity. It may be that Smerdyakov too
was a projection of Ivan's own brain, in spite
of the fact that he was a familiar spectacle in
the town, paid his court to a real Marfa, made
real soups, and murdered a real man. But of
this last we are not quite sure. Certainly
Smerdyakov is as real as Fyodor Pavlovitch,
and as real as Ivan himself ; but so is the
Devil. They are all very real, so very real that
they are in truth a little too real for what we

are provisionally agreed to call reality. That
the people of the town saw Smerdyakov and
did not see the Devil is due perhaps only to the
inevitable awkwardness of representing the
timeless world in time. It may be there really
was no Smerdyakov as there really was no
Devil, and they both had their abode in Ivan's
soul. But then who did the murder ? Then
of course it may have been Ivan himself, or, on
the other hand, there may have been no murder
at all.

The trouble is that all these solutions are
true. Smerdyakov murdered Fyodor Pavlovitch ; Ivan murdered him ; and he was not
actually murdered at all. According as one is
more or less initiate into the grim mysteries
which Dostoevsky practised, he can rest in one
or other of these interpretations. There are
such things, the idealist philosophers tell us,
as degrees of reality. The murder of Fyodor
Pavlovitch might serve as a test case for Mr.
F. G. Bradley. The eighteen-stone trades-
men's wives—and they are the happiest—can
have Smerdyakov for their villain ; the scientific psychologists can have Ivan ; and the
others can find no villain at all, for there was
no murder. Smerdyakov is for those who will
have Dostoevsky an artist, Ivan for those who
will have him a scientist, while for those who

will have him neither of these, but something so strange and terrible that there is as yet no word for it, the thought of a murder will hardly have meaning. . . .

But to return to Smerdyakov and let him be for the moment bodily and actual, sunning himself, even with his hand upon the shoulder of his guitar. Before this mean, contemptible creature Ivan's conscious will is paralysed. Ivan loathes him for his peculiar and revolting familiarity.

With anger and repulsion he looked at Smerdyakov's emasculate sickly face, with the little curls combed forward on his forehead. His left eye winked and grinned as though to say, " Where are you going ? You won't pass by ; you see that we two clever people have something to say to each other."

Ivan shook. " Get away, you miserable idiot. What have I to do with you ? " was on the tip of his tongue, but to his profound astonishment he heard himself say, " Is my father still asleep or has he waked ? "

He asked the question softly and meekly to his own surprise, and at once, again to his own surprise, sat down on the bench. For an instant he felt almost frightened ; he remembered it afterwards. . . .

On that memorable day other things happened which Ivan remembered long afterwards, and they were all connected with Smerdyakov.

" Ivan was fretted, too, by all sorts of strange

and almost surprising desires ; for instance, after midnight he suddenly had an intense inclination to go down, open the door, go to the lodge and beat Smerdyakov. But if he had been asked why, he could not have given any exact reason, except perhaps that he loathed the valet as one who had insulted him more gravely than anyone in the world. On the other hand, he was more than once that night overcome by a sort of inexplicable humiliating terror, which he felt positively paralysed his physical powers. . . . Remembering that night long afterwards, Ivan recalled with peculiar repulsion how he had suddenly got up from the sofa and stealthily as though he were afraid of being watched, had opened the door, gone out on the staircase and listened to Fyodor Pavlovitch stirring down below, had listened a long while—some five minutes—with a sort of strange curiosity, holding his breath while his heart throbbed. And why he had done all this, why he was listening he could not have said. That ' action ' all his life afterwards he called ' infamous,' and at the bottom of his heart he thought of it as the basest action of his life. . . ."

The sickly, emasculate valet had been the cause of no small convulsion in Ivan's soul. Smerdyakov had not only insulted him more grievously than anybody else in the world, but after the insult, Ivan had himself done what he knew in the bottom of his heart was the basest action of his life. Plainly there was contagion in contact with Smerdyakov. Yet if under Smerdyakov's contagion Ivan had debased himself to the lowest, how was it that he could have been insulted by him ? The valet could not have been quite so mean and contemptible after all, for there must have been an unhallowed strength in his vileness and degradation so to have convulsed Ivan's soul. It was as though he had crept into Ivan's being on a sudden, and made his home there.

On the plane of the actual there is but one explanation. Ivan is conniving with Smerdyakov so that Dmitri should murder his father, and will not admit it to himself, yet is he forced to admit it. But the self-deception is extreme and the horror extravagant. One man does not unconsciously *connive* with another ; the activity is one of consciousness. But the horror of all the meetings between Ivan and Smerdyakov is not a horror of the actual world. They are not two conscious, willing beings in contact with one another. When Ivan returned from Moscow, we are told, his hatred for Dmitri grew stronger every day, and " he realised that it was not on account of Katya's ' returns ' that he hated him, but *just because he was the murderer of his father*." Ivan was a clever man—he had Smerdyakov's word for that—but even he was not clever enough to arrive at hating Dmitri for a murder which he himself had planned. He could not so greatly have deceived himself as to whose hands were truly stained with blood. And Dostoevsky did not underline those words from contrariety.

Ivan did not know who did the murder. The conversation with Smerdyakov was to him no more, and no less, than the ugly memory of a terrible dream. It was a dream. When Smerdyakov at last told him by whose bodily hands Fyodor Pavlovitch was slain, Ivan passed by a convulsion of his whole being from the waking world into the dream world again.

" Aren't you tired of it ? Here we are face to face ; what's the use of going on and keeping up a farce to each other ? Are you still trying to throw it all on to me, to my face ? *You* murdered him ; you are the real murderer, I was only your instrument, your faithful servant, and it was following your words I did it."

" *Did* it ? Why did you murder him ? " Ivan turned cold. Something seemed to give way in his brain, and he shuddered all over with a cold shiver. . . .

" Do you know, I'm afraid that you are a dream or a phantom sitting before me ? " he muttered.

" There's no phantom here, but only us two and one other. No doubt he is here, that third, between us. . . ."

At that moment that third is between them, holding them together. The divided soul has been made one again. And Ivan and Smerdyakov are one person, in the dream world which is real. There the slender, flimsy curtain of consciousness which veils himself from Ivan's eyes is rent asunder, and he is one again. His brain stands still with the horror of this sight. He who was so noble a rebel cannot rebel now. He who craved for a being has found one in himself. Stavrogin crushed his instincts, he would allow no other Stavrogin; but how shall this other Ivan be crushed ? How shall his conscious will be asserted; now that he is Ivan no longer, but another ?

Stavrogin had his " monkey," but Ivan's familiar is altogether more terrible. Pyotr Verhovensky was an embodied caricature of his master's superhuman purposes. But between Ivan and Smerdyakov there is no such relation : they are other, absolutely other, yet they are one. Being lies deeper than consciousness, and the self has its tap-roots spread far below in the dark obscenity of things, where the light of consciousness cannot penetrate, and of this strange and awful thing it cannot

even be said that it is or that it lives. There
are no categories for its being, and none can be
invented by the knowing mind which is but a
tiny part of it. For the agonies of consciousness before it no rest nor mollification can be
until the dawn of a new consciousness.

Ivan's being reaches back to the first beginnings of all, though at first he seems to live
wholly under the present Dispensation, his mind
to be our mind, his instincts to be our instincts.
" You are going to perform an act of heroic
virtue," says the Devil to him, " and you don't
believe in virtue." That is an instinct that belongs to our day, the day of two thousand
years, which has been since Christ was made
man. It has been engendered in man's soul by
the law of Love. But there was a Law before
the Christian Law, of an eye for an eye and a
tooth for a tooth, in the age before the word
had been uttered that a man should leave his
father and his brethren, when the father was
the chief and king, his sanctity inviolate and
his authority unquestioned. This law, too,
lives on in the profounder deeps of Ivan's soul ;
he who, loathing his father, had said with the
deliberate intention of his conscious mind :
" Let one reptile devour the other," could not
abide by his word. Even the blood bond of the
old Law which united him in subservience to

his begetter, the loyalty to destroy whose sanc-
tions not Ivan's inhumanly acute and probing
brain was necessary, for it had been done
centuries before his birth, was too strong for
this lover of freedom. Though his mind may
insist that all things are lawful, one thing is
not, and not even in the kingdom of the old
Law is his freedom real. " He hated Mitya
just because he was the murderer of his father.
He was conscious of this and fully recognised
it to himself." Perhaps he might have stood
his ground against the onslaught from the unknown within him, and by recognising that so
much of his soul was based in the past, have
accomplished the miracle that Nikolay Stavrogin died in attempting—to tear himself away
from that whence his being was nourished.
But there are deeper instincts than this, and
these he cannot recognise and live. The Babel
tower of his reason is tumbled at a blow : and
all the anguish of problems unsolved and belief
denied is but a drop in an ocean of pain, when
the veil of his consciousness is suddenly rent,
and the dark and gloomy knowledge comes to
him that there is in him, not only that which
hates the murderer of his unclean father, but
that which by foul and devious ways compassed
his death. The Ivan which listened on the
stairs in the night, and gave to Smerdyakov

not the blow another Ivan would, but sweet words—this self he must behold, and dare not. For this beast is not violent and strong and human, like the hate which goes out of him against Dmitri for his sacrilege, but a creeping thing which crawls and whines and is not man. It is Smerdyakov himself in him : for his actions Ivan can feel nothing of the triumph of the stern and cruel justice that was also in the old time before him, but only everlasting shame. " One reptile has devoured the other," and the devouring reptile is not Dmitri, but in him. The revelation of this beast haunts him not merely with terror, but with the menace of ultimate degradation. Though all things be lawful and his mind cling to that conviction with certainty indubitable, the works of this loathsome and obscene thing are not and can never be. They can never be justified at the bar of his consciousness, for they are not his : he must deny them, although their justification depends upon his acceptance of them. They are his, yet he did not will them ; they are not his, then he is not his. The dilemma is awful and beyond all escaping. His own self is shattered in twain, and worse than shattered, for in spite of denial and his frenzied clinging to his consciousness, a seed has been sown within him of doubt intolerable, whose horror will drive him mad, that this thing is all himself and he is no other.

In Ivan the divided being of man, the rending asunder of those inseparable elements which we call mind and body reaches the last extremity of suffering. It seems even that in him Stavrogin's suffering has been passed, but that is because the anatomy of Ivan's being is more plainly revealed by Dostoevsky's grim and inexorable knife than that of Stavrogin. Alike they stand on the brink of sheer annihilation. Life in them seems to have come to its final and terrible flowering in a consciousness which wills the destruction of the larger life of which it is only a fragment or a form. And in Ivan the most ghastly tragedy of all is revealed. These heroic and terrible spirits who burn out their mortal lives in the superhuman effort to assert themselves, their personalities, their wills, their consciousness, against the universe, who with desperate courage take their stand upon the one firm rock amid the desolate waste of waters, which is their conscious existence, and hurl defiance, even in defeat, at the great whole of which they are members, find at the last that the rock crumbles like sand beneath their feet. They are not themselves, but another. There is neither Being beyond them, nor within them.

Truly, the end is at hand. What remedy or hope of reconciliation can be brought to these minds, which are our own ? If we have not attempted what they have attempted, it is because we are less than they, we are not other than they. They are the perfection of the spirit which is in us. Is there for this spirit a Way of life ?

In Father Zossima's person and teaching, the Way of Christ is put forward in its final and perfect form. No more than at any time before is it the religion of Christianity. The reasoning of an Ivan, which was Dostoevsky's own, had put a barrier for ever between him and a simple faith in the divinity of Christ, the Son of God. Not idly was Father Zossima's orthodoxy suspect to the monks of the monastery ; he, and Dostoevsky with him, was a Christian after the order of Ernest Renan. His teaching is based upon an unbounded reverence for Christ the man. Christ was for him the ideal of human action under the present dispensation ; but the way of Christ was a solution for conduct and not for belief. Perhaps in some words of Kirillov the true nature of Dostoevsky's attitude to Christ is most plainly manifested. On the night when he was to murder himself to assert his self-will in the highest point, because, there being no God, it rested with him to prove

his own divinity, Kirillov cried ecstatically to
Pyotr Verhovensky : —

Listen to a great idea : there was a day on earth,
and in the midst of the earth stood three crosses. One
on the Cross had so much faith that he said to another,
" To-day thou shalt be with Me in Paradise." The
day ended ; both died and passed away and found
neither Paradise nor resurrection. His words did not
come true. Listen : that man was the loftiest of all
on earth. He was that which gave meaning to life.
The whole planet, with everything on it, is mere madness without that man. There never has been any
like Him before or since, up to a miracle. For that
is the miracle, that there never was or never will be
another like Him. And if that is so, if the laws of
nature did not spare even Him, have not spared even
their miracle, and made even Him live for a lie and
die for a lie, then all the planet is a lie and rests on a
lie and mockery. . . .

Yet what man had done he might do again.
He might love all humanity for its suffering,
and take all men's sins upon himself. " Suffering is life," said the Devil. Says Father Zossima : " If the evil doing of man moves you to
indignation and overwhelming distress, even
to a desire for vengeance on the evil-doers, shun
above all things that feeling. Go at once and
seek suffering for yourself as though you were
guilty of that wrong. Accept that suffering
and bear it and you will find comfort. . . ."

FYODOR DOSTOEVSKY

What is this save to still the insurgent consciousness, which demands an answer to the problem of Evil, by the anodyne of pain; and indeed the condition of not wanting a solution is perhaps in itself a solution. But suffering is one thing, and love is another. In *The Journal of an Author* Dostoevsky had let fall a profounder word: "The consciousness that you can bring no help to suffering humanity can change the love you bore it into hatred of that humanity." The way of suffering is easier than the way of love, and Dostoevsky's Christianity proves to be only another "laceration."

But there is a mystical side to Father Zossima's teaching, which, if it was not dearer to Dostoevsky's heart than the way of Christ, was nearer to his thought. Father Zossima's words are saturated with the expectation of the Second Advent, not in any literal, but in a symbolic sense. He does not speak of it outright, as Dostoevsky himself seems hardly to have spoken of it definitely, but the expectation is there.

And can it be a dream that in the end man will find his joy only in deeds of light and mercy, and not in cruel pleasures as now? . . . I firmly believe that it is not, and that the time is at hand. . . . Our people will shine forth in the world, and all men will say: "The

240

stone which the builders rejected has become the head stone of the corner. . . ." "For the sake of the humble and meek the days shall be shortened. . . ."

Like Shatov, Father Zossima believes in the second Advent ; like Shatov, he believes that it will come to pass in Russia. It is easier to ridicule this naïve eschatology than to appreciate the deep metaphysical truth which lies behind the tremendous symbolism of the Apocalypse. To state it in words less awful than those which were given to the apostle in Patmos is to diminish from its significance ; but, since it must be interpreted, the second Advent implies the sudden revelation of a new consciousness, when all eternity shall be gathered into a moment, when there shall be no more division between the body and the soul and no more barriers between the knower and that which is known, when there shall be no more time. The second Advent is the miracle upon which waits the present Dispensation of agony and conflict and sickness and death, for the new consciousness will be a consciousness of harmony. The soul of man will go out into the Universe and be lost and found again, for within it is the seed of a timeless being. Father Zossima's teaching is full of a prescience of that which will be. " Much on earth is hidden from us," he says,

" but to make up for that we have been given a precious mystic sense of our living bond with the other world, the higher heavenly world, and the roots of our thoughts and feelings are not here but in other worlds." Father Zossima speaks to those who have learned to hear, and his language is veiled ; yet it is plain. He hints at a future condition of being when nothing that is hidden shall not be revealed, and the chasm between the timeless world and the world in time spanned at a bound by the new man. That was Dostoevsky's hope : it is not fantastic. Most men have had in their lives some premonition of a new being, of that which by mortality they are not, and yet most truly are. Dostoevsky fought his way to the extreme edge of the knowable, and his latter days were spent peering into the unknown. Into the unknown he flung himself, fevered by the intense strain of poise over the unfathomable. He tried to speak unutterable things, and to fling his imagination into futurity. *The Brothers Karamazov* was his final effort, to bring his hope within his consciousness, to create the symbol of that which is to come.

And the symbol he created is a character utterly unlike all that went before—Alyosha Karamazov. Alyosha in the midst of the welter of his father's swinishness, Dmitri's fever of moral agony and Ivan's torment of the divided person, is, as it were, born good. He is the miracle. Even though he comes to know himself for a sensualist, for the son of his father, and to doubt the God in whom he has unhesitatingly believed, he remained good. Dostoevsky intended to follow his fortunes further, but we know that whatever they might have been, Alyosha will remain positive and whole and good. The trials and doubts which begin to assail him are but the condition of his humanity. However great and overwhelming they be, he has the irrefragable assurance of harmony that he never can forget. He is sure of life and of his own part in it.

But he remains the miracle. It is the quality of miracle that makes him Dostoevsky's hero. In him, through some mysterious alchemy, the clouded and sombre fires of the Karamazov spirit burn with a white pure flame. He is the new, incomprehensible birth; he belongs to the city that is to be in which Dostoevsky, like Shatov, proclaimed through clenched teeth that he would believe. The great spirit which broods over the waters and bears destruction, death and decay in its womb, breaks out at the last into this marvellous flower. It works blindly and beyond the knowledge of man. The great minds that would understand, as

FYODOR DOSTOEVSKY

Dostoevsky had so passionately laboured to understand, end in self-destruction like Stavrogin and Svidrigailov. Dostoevsky knew that their end is inevitable, but deeper than his knowledge he felt that though Stavrogin dies and the light of the human spirit seems to have been quenched life goes on. The death and desolation which attend the searching of the great men who assume the full burden of humanity is not the final word : out of their chaos is born the child who knows.

Thus miraculously, Alyosha is born a lover of humanity. Like a bright flower he springs to the light out of the degradation of his fathers ; like a flower he is free from the torment of earthly personality. His self sweeps with an instinctive movement outward and into the universe, beyond doubts and dialectic to the blinding assurance of eternal harmony. At the moment when he is left most utterly alone, then does his spirit comprehend the world.

He did not stop on the steps either, but went quickly down ; his soul overflowing with rapture, yearning for freedom, space, openness. The vault of heaven, full of soft shining stars, stretched out vast and fathomless above him. The Milky Way ran in two pale streams from the zenith to the horizon. The fresh, motionless, still night enfolded the earth.

The white towers and golden domes of the cathedral gleamed out against the sapphire sky. The gorgeous autumn flowers, in the beds round the house, were slumbering till morning. The silence of the earth seemed to melt into the silence of the stars. The mystery of the earth was one with the mystery of the stars.

Alyosha stood, gazed and suddenly threw himself down on the earth. He did not know why he embraced it. He could not have told why he longed so irresistibly to kiss it, to kiss it all. But he kissed it weeping, sobbing and watering it with his tears, and vowed passionately to love it, to love it for ever and ever. " Water the earth with the tears of your joy and love those tears," echoed in his soul.

What was he weeping over ?

Oh, in his rapture he was weeping even over those stars which were shining to him from the abyss of space, and he was not ashamed of that ecstasy. There seemed to be threads from all those innumerable worlds of God linking his soul to them, and it was trembling all over in contact with other worlds. He longed to forgive everyone and for everything and to beg forgiveness. Oh, not for himself, but for all men, for all and for everything. " And others are praying for me too," echoed again in his soul. But with every instant he felt clearly and as it were tangibly that something firm and unmistakable as that vault of heaven had entered into his soul. It was as though some idea had seized the sovereignty of his mind— and it was for all his life and for ever and ever. He had fallen on the earth a weak boy, but he rose up a resolute champion, and he knew and felt it suddenly at the very moment of his ecstasy. And never, never, all his life long could Alyosha forget that minute. . . .

Alyosha is the only one of all Dostoevsky's characters to whom this consummation is vouchsafed. The others had sought the moment bitterly and with tears, and they found only barrenness and death. Kirillov, maddened by the tyranny of his idea, had a glimpse of this vision in his delirium, and then took his own life to prove that he had attained to the supreme point of self-will. Myshkin himself knew it only in sickness : he was an outcast peering through the gates of heaven, wherein the fly had his part, but not he. But to Alyosha it is given freely. " To him that hath it shall be given : from him that hath not shall be taken away even that which he hath." Dostoevsky's great heart knew too well that to the man who seeks this consummation is denied. It was denied to him. But in spite of denial, he believed ; he could not but believe, even as he could not but disbelieve. He who was Stavrogin, and knew himself for such a man, could not remain in his condition. His soul yearned for the miracle, the process incomprehensible, whereby the weary soul might be born anew and burst forth again upon the world strong in the newness of its spirit.

But he knew that " except the corn of wheat fall into the ground and die, it bringeth not forth fruit." The consummation of belief and full acceptance could come only with a new birth. The life and death of a Stavrogin or a Svidrigailov is the labour pangs of the mind of the world; the pain and chaos of the mighty blind Karamazov spirit strives towards creation by paths which the human consciousness, though working in the light of its extreme incandescence, cannot discover. The force which by its own inward contradiction drives the men of this world to self-annihilation and the void, in another world evolves a mighty youth, from whose open eyes no secrets are hid. From the womb of lust and destruction leaps forth the child of life.

Alyosha belongs to the new world, wherein even the physical being of man is changed. He walks in light, while his brothers are in darkness. Yet his history is blent with theirs. For these things are entwined together—life and its incarnate justification. The other world into which Alyosha was born, neighbours this: the old Adam and the new man must walk hand in hand. And those troubled spirits, Fyodor Pavlovitch, Ivan, Dmitri, Grushenka recognise the virtue that is in the new-born Alyosha; nay, their hopes are set in him. He is an answer to their doubts such as no monastery nor elder, nor even their own seeking could give.

FYODOR DOSTOEVSKY

The creation of this character is the crown of Dostoevsky's final striving to relate by a living symbol that eternal harmony of which Myshkin and Kirillov had glimpses so terrible to the life of doubt and struggle into which those visions burst, like lightning fires. He knew that it was impossible for men of the old Dispensation to bear more than these dread momentary flashes from the world where there is no more time. At those moments, said Kirillov, man must be physically changed or die. Therefore he must die, and be born anew, a shining soul in the new Dispensation. Only thus in the splendour of a new and perfect birth, can mortal eyes look steadily upon the harmony of all things.

This is a hard saying: and here truly is a mystery and a miracle. Yet this is a miracle that must be. The same consciousness which tells us that Stavrogin is the end, tells us also that he cannot be the end; for the consciousness which looks on life and finds it barren, and its end in death, is also the pinnacle, the perfect symbol, of the great process of becoming that denies death. The spirit of man trembles in the last agony of living death, and the consciousness which must deny life has at the last gained the mastery of the body which must affirm. The tyrannous mind will slay the whole of which it is but a part ; and in a Stavrogin, a Svidrigailov or a Kirillov the murder is accomplished. The spirit of man is sick unto death ; and this agony is the final word of the epoch of life in which we live. Though the world of Dostoevsky may seem to us wild and strange, it is ours : he showed forth its being to us in his mighty parables. *The Brothers Karamazov* is the last and greatest of these, for in it Dostoevsky made the super-human effort to hold the past and future together in an eternal present.

The father is the blind force of life, which arose we know not how. It brooded over the face of the waters. Taking the forms of life, high and low, birds of the air and creeping things, obscene, terrible and beautiful, it rose through slime and lust and agony to man. Old Karamazov is life under the old Dispensation. He is a force and no more ; he does not know himself for what he is. He contains within himself the germ of all potentialities, for he is chaos unresolved. He is loathsome and terrible and strong, for he is life itself.

And this old Life is slain by his sons, for by the death of the old Life and the breaking of the old Covenant, the new Life lives and the new Covenant is established. And the form of the new Life that descends upon the chaos

of the father is Christ. Dmitri and Ivan are
divided from the loins of their begetter by the
knowledge of good and evil. That force which
was one and unresolved in their father knows
itself and is divided in them. Dmitri is body
conscious of mind, Ivan is mind conscious of
body. They live under the present Dispensation, as we ourselves have lived and live. In
their life they seek each his consummation.
Ivan spends his being in the tormenting search
for the ultimate resolution of his doubts in
some absolute in which his mind can repose ;
Dmitri his in the quest for the absolute satisfaction of physical love. Yet for all their torment and the force of their passion their desires
are unfulfilled. They cannot be fulfilled. The
body rebels against the final triumph of mind ;
the mind rejects the heaven of the body's
satisfaction. When Ivan in his dream reaches
to the very pinnacle of the seeking of his consciousness, he is overthrown not by the barren
issue of his passionate dialectic, but by the
knowledge that there is that within him which
will not suffer the conclusions of his mind. The
" sticky buds " draw him from the triumph
of his final negation ; the conviction suddenly
rising from his depths, long suspected and long
denied, that in the last recesses of his being is
the beast, or what to the tyrannous mind is

beast-like, makes a mockery of his terrible philosophy.

And Dmitri is overthrown at the end of his tumultuous seeking by the protesting mind. He who was so sure of the beast within him, who could say with such assurance that it was only " some damnable curve " in Grushenka's body that he loved, in a moment comes to the knowledge that it is something else of which he stands in need so passionate. Not all the sexual ecstasies he may compass, not all the dreams of fair women incarnated to do him service, will satisfy him now. That way, too, is barren. It is the " something else " which mocks him in his mad career. This, he knows, will tame the beast and make him beautiful. And in his despair that he will never attain to this and hold it in his grasp, he rides to Mokroe with a case of pistols to " make way." " Are you a driver ? " he says to Andrey while he lashes his galloping horses.

" Then you know that one has to make way. What would you say to a driver who wouldn't make way for anyone, but would just drive on and crush people ? One can't run over a man. One can't spoil people's lives. And if you have spoilt a life, punish yourself. . . . If only you've spoilt, if only you've ruined anyone's life — punish yourself and go away."

That is the despairing voice of the physical man when physical things have failed. His fierce instinct fails him ; a moment has come when he knows it will never satisfy the deeper need, and in that moment he is overthrown. He must bow his head before the power that urges him to the repose which lies beyond all satisfaction of the body. And in those wonderful moments which come before the last mortification of his physical body, when he sits naked and shivering before the blind officers of Law, " particularly loathing the coarse, flat, crooked nail on his right big toe," he has the fulfilment of a moment in the knowledge that he has rejected his old seeking. The ecstasy of the physical body is barren. In his new passionate desire for that which is beyond the body, he can deny the flesh.

" Don't touch me . . . " Grushenka faltered in an imploring voice. " Don't touch me till I'm yours. . . . I've told you I'm yours . . . but don't touch me . . . spare me. . . . With them here, with them close, you mustn't. He's here. It's nasty here. . . ."
" I'll obey you ! I won't think of it. . . . I worship you ! " muttered Mitya. " Yes, it's nasty here. It's abominable."

" Let us be good, not brutes, but good," says Grushenka. And Mitya knows that somewhere in those words is the condition which he seeks. At the last the body fails him, and he too must stand hoping for the miracle, for the rebirth of his divided being into harmony.

So in Ivan and Dmitri is manifest the failure of the divided being of the present Dispensation. The body knows itself for evil, and at the last obeys the bidding of the mind and seeks a good beyond the body. But the good of the mind is the denial of the body. And mind that knows itself for good is at the last confounded by the whisper of the body, and must confess that good is barren without the body and therefore not good at all. Neither body can deny mind, nor mind body ; yet they must deny.

In the story they are reconciled in Alyosha. Alyosha is their mutual victory, the new man. Their father was, Dmitri and Ivan are, Alyosha is to be. Dmitri and Ivan have slain their father, now must they slay themselves. In their death is the beginning of the miracle of the new birth. The present age is ended in suffering and gloom ; from its loins springs forth the new harmony. Alyosha is a perfect being in body, and his mind is in harmony with his body's perfection. He, the actual Alyosha, is only a symbol of what is to come. He has the waking consciousness of the harmony of all things, his heart-strings echo to other worlds.

He will deny nothing. He steps out from the monastery into the world, yet, being in the world, he is not of it, for he walks in the paths of the world to come. His mind tyrannises not over his body, nor his body oppresses his mind. He is a being beautiful, conscious only of his unity, and feeling within himself that which binds him to all humanity, the knowledge that he is the appointed end of all their striving.

Yet he is at the bottom rung of the ladder whereon Dmitri has reached the fourteenth, for he is born out of time. He is a symbol, and he must needs put on the common clay. But these trials will not touch him, for he is secure. He has his consummation, and the knowledge of it will never leave him ; for, though he is clothed in our flesh and lives in our time he belongs to that world wherein " there shall be no more time " and to that order of life when " man must be physically changed." Dostoevsky spoke in parables because the old thought could not define his vision, which is nothing less than the passing away of one phase of the human consciousness and the coming of another. The language of this consciousness is impotent before the vision of the consciousness which is to come.

Nevertheless, *The Brothers Karamazov* is more than a parable, even in its promise, for

that which is to come, also is and has been. It
is eternally. Therefore Alyosha lives and has
his being on this earth and his soul is knit
closely with the things that are here and now.
The miracle of his birth from among the Karamazov foulness is a miracle in time, though
it is wrought by a power which is timeless.
Alyosha is the incarnation of an eternal idea,
yet he is wholly man. What Dostoevsky had
failed to create in Myshkin, he magnificently
achieved in Alyosha. Myshkin was sick;
Alyosha is whole. What Myshkin saw in the
ecstasy of disease, Alyosha beholds with
waking eyes. He is not fashioned, as Myshkin
was, out of the strange delirium of the present
Dispensation, but created new and young and
whole out of the future. Myshkin is built after
the pattern of Christ; he is as it were a *reven-
ant* who looks upon his handiwork after two
thousand years. He has, indeed, no right " to
add ought to that which He did say of old ";
he can do no more to the Grand Inquisitor than
to kiss him upon his bloodless lips. He comprehends that which his words have brought
to pass, but he cannot add to those words : he
can but stroke Rogozhin's head in the silence
of that gloomy house, and mutter incomprehensible words by the unearthly beauty of the
body of the dead Nastasya. He passes back,

silently as he came, into the darkness of the mind, nothing accomplished, no new way shown, no new being lived. He is old and pale and weary.

And Dostoevsky, the mighty conjurer of the mighty dead, was pale and weary too. With the passing of Myshkin, the virtue of Myshkin's archetype passed from the writer's spirit. He brought him back to the earth in the dreadful courage of despair, if haply he, coming again, might be the light of the world once more. But the light was dim by the black darkness which it first had shown ; it was put out by the night itself had created two thousand years ago. The man who feels within himself the incessant hunger and thirst for an answer to his agonising doubts, and has for a moment seen the light of certainty, and after a moment's mad happiness watched it fade away and the old chill despair return—such a man may know a little of the agony of Dostoevsky, when, despite all his hopes and prayers, he first felt within him that the being he had summoned from the dead, and on whose incarnation he had spent his mortal strength, could achieve nothing against the dark forces of the world. This was no mere book tragedy : this was more than a waste of the human spirit. This was the defeat of Christ Himself, in the

mind of one who, even in the depths of the underworld and in defiance of the mind which drove
him to unbelief, obscurely and by devious ways
had put his final trust in Him—not in His
divinity, but in His perfect humanity, as that
of a Man by whom life might yet be guided
and escape destruction. But in the final scene
of *The Idiot* this hope, too, was shattered. For
this was not a writer who bore his books along
to some foregone conclusion. With him, each
of his great final works was a desperate battle-
ground wherein his spirit fought all night long
against despair. He put on the invisible
armour of his last champion Christ, and he was
vanquished. *Victus es, O Galilaee.*

Not out of the past should the victor come,
nor by any means out of the extreme present.
That issue he tried next and most terribly in
The Possessed. But that victory must be his
being could not doubt, even as his consciousness could not escape from vanity and death.
The Brothers Karamazov was the supreme
effort of his life-long struggle. Not out of the
past like Myshkin, not out of the present like
Stavrogin, but out of the future should his last
champion come, Alyosha Karamazov. On this
battlefield, past, present, and future should
strive together ; and though of the great battle
which he foresaw, this time with the light of

triumph in his eyes, mortality cheated him, he had the assurance of victory in the future man. Alyosha was imagined and endured. The gates of hell could not prevail against him. For him, and for him alone, Dostoevsky could throw down the proud challenge of his waking vision. He had seen the harmony of all things, and the knowledge should never pass away from him.

But with every instant he felt clearly and as it were tangibly that something firm and unshakable as that vault of heaven had entered into his soul. It was as though some idea had seized the sovereignty of his mind—and it was for all his life and for ever and ever. He had fallen on the earth a weak boy, but he rose up a resolute champion, and he knew and felt that suddenly at the very moment of his ecstasy. . . .

This Alyosha, the resolute champion, is not a Christian. He has passed beyond the Christian revelation. He is not Myshkin, but Myshkin went to his making, so did Stavrogin, and his brothers and his father. He is that in which their agonies should be justified. He may not believe in God, he may know himself for a sensualist, yet he is not confounded, for his knowledge of the great Oneness needs no belief in God for its support, and the beast which he knows within him is no more a beast. He has transcended these sublunary things.

Their names are but earthly and blunted symbols for the reality which bears within him. He is fair and comely ; his outward bears the impress of his inward harmony ; his body and his spirit together are modulated by the sweet music of other worlds. He is the man who is the promise of all humanity, for whom the old problems are solved by his very being and are not.

EPILOGUE

DOSTOEVSKY believed that the regeneration of mankind rested upon a miracle; and he believed that the miracle was inevitable. It may be said that there was nothing else for him to believe. It is true, and it is also true that the belief of despair is the only one which has a real meaning for the modern world. To believe in that which Dostoevsky believed is to have abrogated nothing of one's humanity; it is rather to have fulfilled humanity.

In this desperate and courageous fulfilment of humanity lies Dostoevsky's greatness. In the speech on Pushkin with which he brought his life to a fitting and symbolic end, he discovered the secret of the poet's greatness in the fact that he was a universal, an " omni-human " man, and he proclaimed that this " omni-human " faculty was the peculiar mark of the Russian genius. Pushkin, he said, had had the power to enter into the souls of other nations than his own and yet had remained original. Rather, his originality lay exactly in his power to submerge himself wholly in the souls of other peoples. He first created, for he first understood, the type of the Russian wanderer over the face of the earth, who seeks not merely a consolation for his personal longings, but happiness for all men. " The Russian wanderer needs the happiness of all men wherein to find his own peace."

That is, perhaps, the most beautiful sentence and the noblest thought in all modern literature. Dostoevsky found this deep desire in the great Russian poet, not only because it was there to be found, but chiefly because it was in himself. In the four years which he spent in The House of the Dead he discovered in himself besides doubt, a great strength. In Siberia, he wrote to his friend Maikov, he had learned that he was a Russian. He then knew that in himself the Russian mind had attained its most perfect manifestation; and at the close of his lifetime of work he proclaimed significantly that the secret of the Russian mind is its universal sympathy.

What he said of Pushkin may be true; but it is truer by far of Dostoevsky himself. His work is a long and desperate battle on humanity's behalf. He took his stand, not on the Russian mind, but on human consciousness itself. What is strange in his work is not the

Russian atmosphere in which it is bathed, but the largeness and grandeur of its scope. He dared to demand that man should be the master of his fate, and in his imagination the loftiest and most terrible thought of the human mind was related directly and inevitably to human action. He refused to believe that man was so little worthy of his humanity that his thought and belief should count for nothing in his life. Every one of his heroes is created out of the truth that man shall not live by bread alone. If man is so builded that he can measure himself against life and struggle with it until death, then he must struggle and, if need be, die. To do less is to be less than man. The true man must have the courage of his mind ; if he does not dare to make his life square with his thought, then is he a traitor to his being. He has denied his humanity and humanity thereby denies him.

Dostoevsky ventured against the unknown with no other armour than human personality. To no writer before him had personality meant so much. He would accept no division in the soul of man. If man could think, then thought was not given to him as a plaything, but to be used, to be trusted and to be obeyed. Where the mind led the being must follow, even if to its own annihilation. He could not conceive that human personality should play traitor to itself.

Dostoevsky believed that this tremendous faith in men's humanity was given to him because he was a Russian. In their turn the Russians claim him as the most Russian of all their great writers. It is not for any English writer to deny the claim. No one who looks steadily upon the nineteenth century can deny that the Russian spirit alone in modern times has taken mankind a great stride nearer to its inevitable goal. In Russian literature alone can be heard the trumpet-note of a new word : other writers of other nations do no more than play about the feet of the giants who are Tolstoi and Dostoevsky, for even though the world knows it not, an epoch of the human mind came to an end in them. In them humanity stood on the brink of the revelation of a great secret.

BIBLIOGRAPHY

The dates given are those of publication, not of composition.

1846. Poor Folk.
      Goliadkin.
      Mr. Prochartschin.
1847. A Novel in Nine Letters.
      The Landlady.
1848. The Stranger-Woman.
      A Weak Heart.
      Christmas and Wedding.
      Bright Nights.
      A Jealous Husband.
1849. Netotchka Nesvanova.
1858. The Little Hero.
1859. My Uncle's Dream.
      Stepanchikovo.
1861. The Insulted and Injured.
      The House of the Dead.
      A Silly Story.
1863. Winter Notes on Summer Impressions.
1864. Letters from the Underworld.
1865. An Unusual Happening.
      Crime and Punishment.
1866. The Gambler.
1868. The Idiot.
1870. The Eternal Husband.
1871. The Possessed.
1873. The Journal of an Author (first sixteen chapters).
1875. A Raw Youth.
1876-7. The Journal of an Author.
1877. The Little Girl.
1879-80. The Brothers Karamazov.
1880. The Speech on Pushkin.